THE SCHOOL REFORM HANDBOOK

THE SCHOOL REFORM HANDBOOK

How to
IMPROVE
your SCHOOLS

By JEANNE ALLEN with Angela Dale

The Center For Education Reform
Washington, DC

© Copyright 1995 by The Center for Education Reform,
    1001 Connecticut Ave., NW, Suite #920, Washington, DC 20036

Cover Design by Yvonne W. Pover
Graphic Design by Carol L. Nansel

Library of Congress Card Catalog Number 95-68282

ISBN 0-9646028-0-6

To the teachers,

without whom civilization would surely perish.

And to the parents,

our children's first teachers.

TABLE OF CONTENTS

Section I: What is School Reform?

Section II: Who's in Charge: The Education Establishment

Section III: Working For Reform

Acknowledgments

Since the very beginnings of The Center for Education Reform, not a day has passed without calls from people in "the real world," with real world concerns about how their schools are doing, how their children are doing, and what they can be doing to make a difference in education. The School Reform Handbook grew out of our commitment to help every one of our callers address his or her particular concerns, and to help them create lasting opportunities and organizations dedicated to addressing those concerns.

The School Reform Handbook, and indeed The Center, would not have been possible without several key people and organizations and countless individuals dedicated to seeing our work flourish.

Angela Dale — for her dedication and commitment. Angela provided information, excellent writing and editing, and a keen eye to what the final product should look like. Her prior work in both publishing and television industries is a rare commodity, and added creativity and foresight She is a friend and a colleague, to whom I am deeply indebted, not only for her work on this project, but for her dedication to the Center and its goals.

Overall, the progress of school reform owes greatly to the efforts of Jerry Hume, our Board Chairman, who not only contributes his valuable time, energy and resources to us, but whose keen sense of the world of reform and unwavering commitment to education push us ever forward. Indeed, each and every member of The Center's Board has been a tremendous source of wisdom and support.

This book has also been made possible by the generous support of the philanthropic community, including The John M. Olin Foundation, The Walton Family Foundation, and The J.M. Foundation. Each of these organizations was daring enough to put its money on a relatively new horse, on the basis of strongly-held ideas and intentions. For their vote of confidence we are grateful.

A small band of warriors at The Center provided invaluable support. Most critical to the end product was Michael Barrett, himself a former inner city teacher, whose research, editing and passion for reform helped define the Handbook. Nora Roach continued to keep The Center and its staff on course from day to day, even in the face of intense activity on this and other projects simultaneously. Few groups are as lucky to have as competent an intern as Karla Hogarth. And without Shelby Lamm's copy editing, we'd be no where near finished.

Thanks, too, to the dedicated people in the hundreds of thousands of school buildings across America determined to succeed despite often intimidating odds, and to the education reformers – including many of our dedicated friends throughout the states, such as Jim Amann, Tracy Bailey, Tim Barth, Pam Benson, Polly Broussard, Yvonne Chan, Milo Cutter, Paul DeWeese, Sean Duffy, Lisa Graham, Ted Kolderie, Thaddeus Lott, Ed McMullens, Susan Mitchell, Dennis Odle, Jim Rubens, Fawn Spady, Fritz Steiger, Lil Tuttle, Chris Yelich, Karen Zondlo – and to those tireless reporters whose honest work sheds light on those efforts and make it clear that good reforms are taking root.

And finally, deep gratitude must go to John C. Allen, whose support, outstanding work, advice and unparalleled communications savoir-faire have built The Center and guided this effort.

Introduction

e Americans cherish our educational tradition. We have always
been able to measure the success of our country and our culture
by the character of our schools.

But nothing is perfect.

The schools are in a constant state of reform. In the process, they have
not measured up to our needs nor our standards. Sadly, the quality of our
schools has declined. Now the call for real, meaningful reform is growing
louder. In a time of growing competition from abroad and social upheaval
at home, more Americans are demanding to know why, and more important, what can be done.

How bad is it? SAT scores have declined so dramatically in the last
thirty years that scores are being readjusted along a curve to make students
look better. Nationally, less than three-quarters of high school freshmen
graduate in four years.[1] In an urban setting this number drops to less than
half.[2] Of those who do finish, more than half of twelfth grade graduates
leave with restricted abilities in reading and math.[3] And that doesn't
account for the nearly one million students who already have dropped
out.[4]

Remember the words to that old favorite song, "School Days: When
We Were a Couple of Kids?"

"School days, school days, dear old golden rule days. Reading and 'rit-
ing and 'rithmetic ...."

These words are not merely nostalgic, but words that still ring true for
many of us. Most of us *do* believe that the schools should be teaching the 3
R's first and foremost. And most of us would like to believe that our schools
are safe havens for our little ones.

But in reality, too many children leave school without knowing even
the basics in reading, writing and math, let alone history, science and literature. Stories about metal detectors being installed and children carrying
guns and knives are all too common. This might seem incredulous to some.
Others may simply ignore such reports because, perhaps, they think their

school is fine. There *are* extraordinary people working in the schools daily to make sure our children are well-educated and safe. But that is not always the case, and today schools that excel are the exception, not the rule. Those who continue to believe everything is A-OK would be truly stunned to discover just how far away the schools have gotten from the business of educating.

That is why parents, teachers, businesses and civic leaders nationwide have begun to demand changes. From community to community across the country, a true grass roots movement has sprung up to bring back control and excellence to our schools. Independent charter schools are starting up, businesses are joining with schools to bring innovative programs to children, and foundations are reaching out to those less fortunate to provide them with a solid education and a sound future. A new level of accountability is being demanded of schools as they come under closer scrutiny from parents, educators and communities actively determined to repave the road education will take into the twenty-first century.

What do Americans think about their educational system?

The 26th Phi Delta Kappa/Gallup education poll shows that too many are less than satisfied, but more are getting involved on a local level to do something about it. Here are some of the 1994 Gallup Poll's findings:

What Americans think:

◆ 51% gave their local public schools a grade of C, D, or Fail.

◆ 72% gave the nation's public schools a grade of C, D, or Fail.

◆ 29% gave the public school attended by their oldest child a grade of C, D, or Fail.

◆ 37% believe their community's public schools have gotten worse in the last five years, up from 30% in 1990 and 19% in 1988.

◆ 51% believe that public schools in the nation as a whole have gotten worse in the last five years.

◆ 15% believe that the public school attended by their oldest child has gotten worse in the last five years.

◆ Over 90% believe that values such as respect for others, industry or hard work, fairness in dealing with others and civility or politeness should be taught in school. The 1993 Gallup Poll indicated that over 90% felt that traits such as democracy, honesty, patriotism, moral courage and the golden rule should be taught in school.

◆ Over 75% believe that there should be more emphasis in high school on math, English, and science. Almost 90% believe high schoolers could be learning more math and science than they do now.

◆ 54% believe charter schools are good for education.

What Americans are doing about it:

◆ 28% attended a meeting dealing with the local public school situation, up from 16% in 1991 and 10% in 1983.

◆ 20% attended a meeting to discuss school reforms being proposed.

◆ 16% attended a school board meeting, up from 7% in 1991 and 8% in 1983.

◆ 15% served as a member of a school related committee.

◆ 87% of public school parents met with a teacher or administrator of a local school about their child. This was up from 77% in 1991 and 62% in 1983.[5]

THE SCHOOL REFORM HANDBOOK

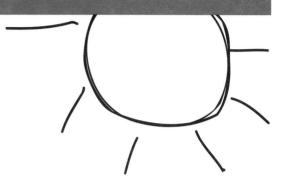

What is School Reform?

1: A Look at School Reform

The idea of education reform is not new, and reforms and reformers have come and gone. Some have made a career out of championing every new educational fad in the name of reform. But, in the face of such prolific and public "reform" activities, America's public schools essentially have remained unchanged in the way they deliver education and the manner in which they are organized. The schools have fallen behind the rest of the country's march into the future. The schools have resisted change, resulting in their increasing inability to educate American children.

The reform movement that is gaining momentum and support is aimed deeper than the efforts of years past. It is rooted in a fundamental reevaluation of the way schools do business. Dedicated reformers believe that those who have traditionally controlled education are responsible for today's stagnant, immovable system, and as a result they are being asked to step aside. "The blob," as former U.S. Secretary of Education William Bennett so aptly dubbed them in a 1987 report on America's schools, has claimed exclusive dominion over issues of reform for too long. Although claiming to make a lot of changes, the establishment has only repackaged the same old programs and structures, while protecting their power base. Some perpetual "reformers," such as those who run the administration offices, talk loosely of "real systemic reform." However, their tough words are often just more camouflage for bureaucratic shell games. Unions, administrators and even some school boards are staunch defenders of the status quo. Sadly, their greatest stake in the system is not the children but their own jobs. And the less the system changes, no matter how badly needed, the more secure their jobs. (More on this in Section II: Who's In Charge?)

For parents with children going through that status quo system, or communities and businesses hiring the graduates of that system, such tinkering has spurred outrage and action. They know that our children are our future, and nothing short of dynamic, immediate, systemic reform offers any possibility for revitalizing education in America.

Meaningful Reform

It was in 1983, with the release of the report "A Nation At Risk," that this movement began to stir. That report brought national attention to the "rising tide of mediocrity" pervading the educational system.[1] This was a system churning out children under-educated and ill-equipped to survive in our world. The report reaffirmed that new money and new programs, while indisputably keeping the United States at the top of industrial nations in academic spending, did not produce better-educated students.

The decline of education and the need for reform soon gained unprecedented prominence across the country among policy makers, community leaders, educators and parents. In the states, the governors began to reexamine the policy and practice of their school systems. As traditional reform efforts continued to yield only marginal results, the focus shifted toward a complete rethinking of the entire public education system, which had not changed substantially in the more than 100 years since its foundation. There was a renewed cry for accountability, as parents, communities and the nation tried to get a handle on just how and what their kids were learning in school. But little actually happened.

It is important to understand that people have been trying. Throughout the 1980s, in particular, there were reports, Governors' summits, educators' summits, and summits about summits. Each meeting produced widespread agreement that reform should no longer be about which new programs or how much new money could improve schools. The talk was moving away from that exclusive focus on "inputs." Instead, consensus was forming that we must begin to assert our collective energies on measuring how well schools do and requiring that certain standards be met.

Meanwhile, landmark research[2] ushered in the 90s with the bold realization that simply requiring more of the present system is not enough to save the schools. What makes for a responsive school - one that works - is a combination of several factors: high expectations by parents and schools; smaller schools - not the sprawling, shopping-mall type one sees so often today; strong leaders; and consumer choice. If parents could actively choose which schools their children attend, a child could have a more successful academic experience; the idea of school choice could provide the solid first step toward reintroducing accountability and excellence to the schools. And the facts soon bore this out. Programs that permit parents a wide array of choices already have been responsible for great strides. The following examples show the evolution of school reform and demonstrate how far we've come from the tinkering of days gone by:

◆ In Harlem, a choice system among the public schools has been successfully underway since 1974. Acting on their desire to create and work in smaller schools that were more responsive to their community, teachers launched a handful of schools-within-schools in East Harlem's District 4. The innovation led to a rise in the district's reading scores from dead last to 15th among the city's 32 districts. Every parent in the district can and must choose which high school their child will attend, and more than a thousand students from outside the district every year seek enrollment in one of District 4's schools.[3]

◆ A state-wide choice program in Minnesota has enjoyed similar success and support. In 1985, the state began giving parents the option to send their children to any public school in the state. A post-secondary enrollment program allows high schoolers to attend college for dual credit. By the 1992-93 school year, at least 15% of Minnesota students chose a school other than the one assigned by their district.[4] Among the alternatives are Minnesota's various "second chance" options, which each year get thousands of at-risk students, including teenage parents, students with substance abuse problems and underachievers, back in school.

◆ In Milwaukee in 1991, Assemblywoman Polly Williams, herself a mother and grandmother struggling and frustrated with the city's failing public schools, directed the Parental Choice Grant Program through the Wisconsin legislature. This school choice program, the first to include private institutions, freed parents to choose for the first time from among qualified schools outside the entrenched, beleaguered Milwaukee public school system.

◆ In 1993 Puerto Rico enacted a far-reaching school choice program which permitted poor children to attend any public, private or parochial school. In one year the number of children participating increased almost ten-fold, to approximately 17,000. In the 1994-95 school year, 88% chose a public school and 12% chose a private school.[5]

◆ Private organizations in Indianapolis and other cities across the country have begun tuition scholarship programs to allow underprivileged families the opportunity to send their children to their school of choice.

Children in these programs are more enthusiastic about school, have better attendance rates and are performing well in their chosen school.

◆ In states such as Minnesota, Arizona and Wisconsin students not served by their public schools can opt into specially designed private programs. In December 1993, Minneapolis contracted with a private firm to serve as the district's superintendent of schools. A private organization also went under contract with the cities of Baltimore, Maryland and Hartford, Connecticut in 1993 and 1994 to manage and maintain some or all of their public schools. Other districts bring in private companies to provide remedial programs.

◆ One of the newest and fastest growing means of school improvement in the 90s are the charter schools opening up in states across the country. Such schools grow directly out of the pressing needs of their communities and operate relatively free from the multitude of regulations which plague their district counterparts. Each school's teachers must choose to work there; parents of children must choose to enroll them and often are required to contribute their own time and support to the school; and local businesses and community groups often volunteer their resources and expertise to ensure the school's success. Charters are public schools which are permitted to operate much like private schools.

◆ Nationally, 2,400 magnet schools offer specialized programs to families in areas that have found it difficult to desegregate their schools. Approximately 1.2 million students attended magnet schools in 1993.

Each individual success story among the variety of examples here makes it clear that all schools could benefit from some shaking-up. One million children are taking advantage of new choices made possible by meaningful school reform options; two million benefit from a wider scope of reform efforts.

Part and parcel of a real school reform movement is the fact that there is no single solution for any child or any school. The best fundamental reforms will be shaped to the needs of each community. The success of such reforms will be judged by their ability to hold schools strictly accountable for results, to involve and be responsive to parents and the community and to cut schools loose from the bureaucracy that is so stifling to them now.

The actual progress made in a few years is remarkable. As of January 1, 1995, 6 states had charter school laws granting a healthy amount of freedom from regulations, with another 5 providing for some limited charter opportunities.[6] By early 1995, more than 140 charter schools were up and running in California, Minnesota, Colorado, Michigan and

"Scrambling Education Reformers: A Teacher's View"

Twenty years into an increasingly debilitated education reform movement, we are still forming task forces, working on reports and mandating everything but the kitchen sink - with precious little to show in the way of practical action or results. Our youngsters at every level, mine included, fall further and further behind. Tests and test scores comprise a sad, long-running joke, even as our children are condemned to a curriculum that teaches them how to do almost nothing.

Rather than marching into our schools some fall to demand that students write in complete, grammatically correct sentences and that parents supervise study time every school night, we're still organizing that Education Reform notebook.

Example: The Colorado Department of Education is already up to here in a state-mandated program called standards-based education. Once you get around the educationese, standards simply means that your kid better darn well be able to do some basic things like reading, writing, computing and listening ....

Time to get honest. We educators can't even begin to do all the things we've promised these past 20 years. Ain't no way. In last Sunday's column, my editorial boss, Chuck Green, said that folks don't listen to, or trust, politicians because they lie. So do educators: We lie to our public, our parents, our students, even ourselves. We don't mean to. It's just that we want so badly to please everybody, and there's the rub. Real learning hurts feelings. If they're really learning, our children inevitably find out that they're not the center of the universe; that they're not infallible; that their group doesn't rule the ant hill; that their lives and ours are eked out in the "valley of tears," and that mastery of any academic subject demands endless hours, days and years of blood, sweat and tears. There are no shortcuts.

Still, we educators are scared to say, "Mr. and Mrs. Smith, your 10th grade son is an illiterate. He cannot write legibly or clearly, listen to either written or spoken directions, or put his ideas or opinions into written form." We're terribly frightened we'll be blamed by his parents, by politicians and talk show hosts.[7]

Jefferson County middle school teacher
Craig Bowman

A Look At Student Achievement

The following are highlights of trends in student achievement in America. Clearly, too many students are not being challenged to meet high standards or given a learning environment that will prepare them to be strong citizens and skilled workers.

◆ Only 71% of all students entering ninth grade graduate four years later.[8] Less than half of students in urban schools graduate in four years.[9]

◆ The current status dropout rate for young adults ages 19-20 is about 14%.[10] (In Japan it's 9%; in Germany, 11%.) The dropout rate for Blacks is 15%.[11] For Hispanics, the rate is 36%.[12] 30% of children from low-income families have dropped out by the time they're 19 or 20.[13]

◆ U.S. students spend less than half their school day, or about 3 hours, on core academic subjects[14] – in Germany and Japan, students spend almost twice as much time on such subjects.[15] Although U.S. students spend more time at school (about 1,000 hours a year) than their counterparts in Japan and Germany,[16] that time is being taken up by non-academic pursuits such as gym, driver's education and counseling.

◆ In the last twenty-two years, national average SAT scores have decreased 35 points.[17] The average math score has dropped to 479 and the average verbal score has sunk to 423.[18] The percentage of students who score above 600 on the verbal portion of the test has slipped from 112,530 in 1972 to 73,080 in 1993, a 36% drop.[19]

◆ Only 25% of fourth graders, 28% of eighth graders and 37% of twelfth graders reach or exceed a proficient level of reading.[20] 41% of fourth graders, 31% of eighth graders and 25% of twelfth graders don't even have the "basic" reading skills for their grade level. Less than 5% of elementary and secondary students reach an advanced level of reading ability in school.[21]

◆ Three-quarters of United States students, tested in grades 4, 8 and 12, are not proficient in math.[22] Half of twelfth graders were unable to solve problems that involve fractions, decimals or percents, or that draw on elementary concepts in geometry, statistics or algebra.[23]

◆ Only one-third of eleventh graders could identify, on a multiple choice test, in which half century the Civil War was fought. Less than 40% could identify the purpose of the Emancipation Proclamation, and fewer than two-thirds knew the significance of Brown v. Board of Education.[24]

Wisconsin. Private choice scholarship programs were serving over 8,500 students in 20 cities throughout the nation, with equal numbers on waiting lists from California to Georgia. Districts in 17 states were contracting with private companies to provide educational services ranging from foreign language instruction to remedial reading to the operations of an entire school or school district. 11 states had open enrollment programs allowing students to attend a school in any district in the state, and 8 states offered post-secondary enrollment options so that high school students could simultaneously attend college and fulfill their high school graduation requirements.[25]

The November 1994 election also revealed an astonishing trend. Victorious candidates for governor in most states declared their full-fledged support for reforms that return local control to the people. In addition, a new breed of state superintendent began to emerge, making it even more probable that school improvement would extend beyond the two million children it already was helping. There are still many obstacles, as the next few chapters will make clear. But learning what and who they are, and facing them head on, will be the first step toward getting the schools you want and your children deserve.

2: Models for School Reform

Reform can happen anywhere. From inner-city New York to suburban Charlotte, North Carolina, programs are operating that put schools and parents back in the driver's seat for their children's education. The following are descriptions of successful models of reform that are gaining support and acclaim in neighborhoods and cities across the country. This will provide you with a brief outline of how and why these reforms work and show some of the struggles and triumphs that are shaping the reforms and reformers of today and tomorrow.

Choices in the Public Schools

Beginning with the magnet schools that emerged from the desegregation orders of the sixties and seventies, educators, parents and legislators have recognized that to get a good education, students need to go to good schools. While magnet schools focused on maintaining ethnic balances through things like forced busing, which has had questionable results, their focus on creating an atmosphere of excellence and opportunity, to voluntarily attract a diverse school population, has thrived. The competition to get into these schools is fierce (often determined by lottery), and standards and achievement are high. In 1993, approximately 1.2 million children attended more than 2,400 magnet schools - triple the number in 1983.[1]

With the success of these magnets, some districts and states have recognized the need and desire of parents to actively pick their children's school and the benefit such involvement brings to both families and schools. The magnets have created various levels of choice for their communities, in some cases allowing

John and Jeannie Price wanted their kindergartner to go to the magnet school close to their Little Rock home so badly back in 1988 that they put their house up for sale and moved to North Little Rock to improve their daughter's odds of getting in.

Before they moved, the school told them that while they were 32nd on the waiting list, they might be able to get her in by the 5th grade. The popularity and the success ... of the magnet and specialty programs have spawned an additional 23 other such schools of choice over the past 12 years ....

John Price spent two nights in his sleeping bag on a chaise lounge in front of the North Little Rock School District administration building so he could be among the first in line for magnet school registration.[2]

students to pick between the schools of a district, to transfer into a nearby district, or even choose from any school in the state. While the existence of such programs doesn't guarantee that children have access to a top-notch education, it certainly increases their odds, and nudges schools to try harder to attract students.

> "Research suggests that when parents and students are involved in school choice, achievement occurs at a higher level than when they are not involved."[3]
>
> *Little Rock Superintendent*
> *Henry Williams*

Open enrollment is another choice option now in place. When open enrollment was introduced in Los Angeles in the fall of 1993, parents eagerly began to search for the perfect school; with 22,000 seats open in the district, schools eagerly put their best foot forward to bring parents on board. Florida launched a post-secondary enrollment option, allowing high school students to attend local colleges for high school and college credit, and over 25,000 students currently participate. In the urban school districts of Boston, Massachusetts (enrollment: 60,000), Indianapolis, Indiana (enrollment: 47,000), and Detroit, Michigan (enrollment: 50,000), parents must choose a school for their child. In fact, in Boston, 57% of students now choose non-local schools. And the competition among schools trying to attract students has forced schools to be more informative to parents and to offer a better product. States including Ohio, Utah, Nebraska and Iowa allow open enrollment across the state. Thousands of students take advantage of inter-district transfer programs in states including Colorado, Arkansas, Tennessee, Washington and Idaho.

> "My daughter was about ready to drop out of high school at age 16 and become a drummer in a rock band. I knew she had talent. But high school wasn't working for her. I heard about the new program (in Minnesota) which allows high school students to take college courses, and asked her to try it. Two years later she simultaneously graduated from high school and completed her first two years of college, with a high "B" average. Stacy had the ability to succeed, but without an alternative I am convinced she would not have graduated."[4]
>
> *A Minnesota Mom*

Critics often complain that school choice reforms cater to educated parents and smart kids and will actually hurt the kids who need the most help. That is certainly not the case in East Harlem's District 4, or in two other noteworthy schools of choice for New York City youth. Any city high schooler can attend the Wildcat Academy, but the majority of the 120 students currently choosing it were truants at their assigned school, and 25% are on probation or parole. These troubled teens who felt lost in the city's larger, more anonymous high schools are now more likely to show up from day to day at the smaller school. Wildcat boasts an 85% attendance rate versus a 77% rate at other alternative high school degree programs. "I know I could leave, but they make learning fun," says student Jasmine Bruno.[5]

Another choice for some New York youth - those faced with a prison sentence, generally substance abusers or drug offenders - is the residential Phoenix Academy outside New York City. Students can choose to attend the school instead of serving jail time. Said Justice Richard Butcher, of the State Supreme Court in Queens, "It takes a lot of determination to succeed in this program." State Supreme Court Justice Burton Roberts said, "It's not going to work 100 percent of the time, but I think it will work with greater frequency and much more effectiveness than merely sending them to a penal institution."[6]

Half-hearted "reform" measures, such as school-based management (SBM), often lack the true autonomy found in these successful, alternative schools. SBM has been promoted by many education groups as offering sufficient flexibility and autonomy within schools to bring about reform and improvement without the broader mechanisms for parental choice. However, judging by the experience of Dade County, Florida, SBM often leads to petty infighting, where teachers are trying to innovate without having the autonomy to make their own decisions. Unlike charter schools that are legally free from regulations, schools operating under SBM and local school councils often find themselves subject to more regulation, rather than less, as varying factions try to institute control.[7]

Charter Schools

The advent of charter schools has given parents and teachers the opportunity to roll back regulations, roll up their sleeves and create and operate schools in which they want to teach and send their children. A charter school must practice open admission policies, meet health and safety standards, and comply with civil rights laws, but is *not* bound to state education regulations over curriculum, personnel, scheduling and financial administration. In exchange for these waivers, a charter school must show satisfactory achievement by its students, as equal to or above the state's average student achievement. Other basic goals of a charter may include reducing dropout rates or increasing the number of students placed in a job

Key Elements in a Charter Bill

As charter school proposals gain momentum, it is important to stay committed to an ideal while focusing on the practical issues of bringing these new schools to life. Any new law or bills should be compared to this charter school model:[8]

A. Purpose

Improve pupil learning

Increase educational choices for pupils

Create new professional opportunities for teachers

Establish a new accountability for schools

Encourage the use of various, innovative learning methods

B. Formation

Charter schools may be formed by:

      1) creating a new school

      2) converting an existing school

C. Organizer

Proposals may be made by an individual or organization, including parents, teachers and non-profit education groups

D. Sponsor

Sponsors may include:

      1) the district school board

      2) the state board of education (or state superintendent)

      3) the board of a public post-secondary institution

E. Legal Entity

The charter will be a separate entity, not legally a part of the district

F. Accountability

Performance reports will be made to the sponsor and immediately become public documents

G. Teachers

Teachers may choose to be employees of the school

Bargaining units will be separate from other units

H. Renewal or Termination

At the end of the charter, sponsors may choose not to renew on any of the following grounds:

      -Failure to meet required student performance

      -Violation of law

      -Irresponsible financial management

or college upon graduation. While charters typically last five years, status can be revoked at any time for violations or if the school is not performing as promised.

A driving force behind the implementation of charter laws in a number of states is the desire to increase the amount and variety of schools available to educate disadvantaged children and those at risk of dropping out of school altogether. With the increased freedom and flexibility of charter schools, teachers, parents and communities can start schools that directly address the special needs of their children and provide options to children who may benefit from a school that operates outside the traditional factory model.

Charter schools that receive operating funds directly from the state can cut out layers of expensive district bureaucracy. And innovations in curriculum, scheduling and service delivery become possible when the funds to implement them are tied to results rather than procedures. For example, The Vaughn Next Century Learning Center in Los Angeles realized a $1.2 million surplus its first year as a charter school. During that 1993-94 year, the school maintained a 99% attendance rate, reduced class sizes, hired new teachers and added a computer lab and a teacher resource center. The school was able to use the year's savings to improve and expand its facilities.[10]

Some of the charter schools approved in Massachusetts in March, 1994, to open in September, 1995, include: a boarding school for homeless children, headed by a retired rear admiral; a back-to-basics school focusing on the three R's, founded by a group of parents; a school for high school dropouts run by a community college. "Most of the proposals address the needs of the child not able to succeed in current public schools," said Piedad Robertson, the state's Education Secretary.[9]

The most strident opposition to charter schools comes from pockets of the education establishment. Some charter laws give local school boards the authority to grant or deny charters in their district. However, some boards view charter schools as competition and are unwilling to give up control over funds and operating decisions. They fear, perhaps rightfully so, that successful charter schools will make district schools look poor by comparison. While teachers across the country are highly enthusiastic about the prospects of charter schools for themselves and their students, their representative bodies, the teachers unions, have proven to be some of the most vocal and vested opponents to this movement. For instance, the Michigan Education Association, at 127,000 members one of the largest and richest unions in the country, spent $2 million advertising against Michigan's charter bill and its chief sponsor, Governor John Engler. Nevertheless, the bill passed at the end of 1993. The teachers union then turned its attention to the courts, where it challenged the constitutional standing of the Michigan charter school law, a law which benefits its members directly by allowing teachers to start their own public schools.[11]

In another perverse twist of logic, the Sacramento City Teachers Association, in conjunction with the California Teachers Association, filed a grievance, on procedural grounds, against the Bowling Green Elementary charter school because it reduced class sizes from 33 to 25 – despite the fact that this is the sort of workplace change the unions are always demanding. The union also complained because Bowling Green's charter allows the school to fill teaching positions based on merit, rather than seniority, and accused the school of circumventing collective bargaining agreements in its personnel policy. All this, even though California law purposely exempts charter schools from such agreements on the grounds that the freedom will improve schooling.

Systemic reforms like charter schools offer many benefits - not only to parents but to the community. In particular, these schools can have a positive competitive effect on how money is spent. When Bowling Green used an outside supplier to get lower prices on paper goods, the district responded by lowering its own prices - giving a price break to all its schools. Districts are not always receptive to such savings, however. When Bowling Green found a private contractor who would carpet its special education building at less than half the cost of the district's bid, the two district departments that were going to fund the carpet balked. They claimed the private contractor was providing an inferior product, despite indications to the contrary. Bowling Green had to go without new carpets.

> "For years I'd been thinking that there had to be a different way to teach. I was stuck in a rut: five classes a day, lasting 55 minutes. But then I got a chance to help develop the Minnesota Center. It's been a lot of hard work, but I never wanted to go back. For me, this is the right way to teach - interdisciplinary, with a team of teachers, with large blocks of time, and a group of students who've chosen to work with us."[12]
>
> *Minnesota Center teacher*
> *Gary Christofferson*

Entrepreneurial Partnerships and Contracting

The use of private contractors, particularly for support services, has become popular among public schools who want to reduce costs, eliminate waste and concentrate more resources on educating children. Non-instructional and support services eat up more than 40% of public-education spending nationwide.[13] For example, the superintendent of the Piscataway, New Jersey public school district began contracting for bus and food service and saved $2 million a year. Such competition is spurring districts to reduce their own costs to schools for services they provide. The Peoria Unified School District in Arizona saved about $250,000 when it first started contracting for custodial services in 1991 and enjoyed cleaner schools as a result. Then the district's own custodial service delivery, which used to cost at least 25% more than contracted services, reduced its service to within 5% of the outside contractor's costs.[14]

Federal, state and local government agencies are turning more and more to the private sector for goods and services as a cost saving measure in the face of bureaucracy budget crises. School districts are contracting out most often for transportation, maintenance and food services, a trend that emerged significantly in the last five years. Of the 100 largest school bus fleets around the country, 40% is operated by private contractors. In a survey by the Illinois Education Association, more than 45% of 360 responding school districts contract out for one or more services.[15]

Public school systems are also experimenting with contracting free-lance teachers and educational services to handle both remedial and classroom teaching. Options for Youth (OFY), based in Los Angeles, educates dropouts at their homes through contracts with the local school district. This benefits both the school districts and the students: the districts are permitted to "reinvent" the student and receive the daily funding for each child that would otherwise be lost, and students are given a second chance to succeed outside the environment in which they failed. Options for Youth has educated about 1,500 dropouts annually since it began in 1987. The program gives districts a money-back guarantee - if the students do not meet their grade level criteria, OFY does not collect funds. The majority of OFY students are minorities, and 40% of them are teen mothers. A majority of enrollees are reported to continue their education after the program and advance to higher education.[16]

> " I have to tell my kids "no" a lot. I know every kid in town wants a designer pair of pants or the most expensive shoes in town. Mine do without. Not only that, but we don't get to eat what we want. There's been many times I went to the grocery store with $20 and that was supposed to last the whole week."
>
> *Mother, Indianapolis*

> "[My child] is doing excellent in her new school. Her grades and attitude have made a change for the best. She likes school a lot more, and she looks forward to going to school every day. Without PAVE [Partners Advancing Values in Education] I would not have been able to send her to a private school."
>
> *Parent, Milwaukee*

> " The curriculum makes all the difference as he is now being academically challenged. There is no comparison to the public school, it is totally different. What you are doing at the CEO [Children's Educational Opportunity Foundation] is not in vain. Ricky has a better chance of receiving the education he deserves."
>
> *Parent with two children in choice schools, Austin*
> *(She works for the local school district and declined further comment on the public schools.)*

Another independent organization, Ombudsman Education Services, contracts with districts in seven states to educate students who are in danger of dropping out of the system for academic and behavioral reasons. Ombudsman receives $3,000 to $4,000 per enrolled student - well below the average $5,000 to $8,000 per student these states spend in the public schools - yet boasts an 85% success rate with the district's most difficult students.[17] Throughout the year, Ombudsman enrolls over 3,000 at-risk students from more than 100 school districts.[18]

Some districts have gone a step further and contracted with private companies to take over part or all of a school system, with the goal of improving both academic and financial management of the public schools. Baltimore City Public Schools, for example, contracted with Education Alternatives, Inc. (EAI) to manage nine of its public schools, a move which has resulted in better maintained, better attended schools. EAI claims it has been able to reduce administrative and overhead expenditures by 25%. As a result, although EAI and other schools receive the same amount of funding from the district, about $5,918 per student, EAI is able to spend $1,100 more per student directly in the classroom. In one EAI school, the attendance rate has hit 98%, up from 90% the previous year, and well-above the district's 92% average.[19]

The Hartford, Connecticut, school board also contracted with EAI to handle the day-to-day operations of the district's 32 schools. In Minneapolis, the school board hired an independent company to serve as the superintendent of its district. The company is paid only after it successfully meets various performance objectives set by the board.

Parental Grant and Choice Scholarship Programs

For some poor families, school choice means being able to choose not only from among district schools but from among independent schools. In Milwaukee, Assemblywoman Polly Williams crusaded to help youngsters from low-income homes receive grants to attend nonsectarian private schools in the city. For the 1993-94 school year, 733 students received $2,970 to cover tuition at any one of 13 qualifying schools.[20] Despite the objections of education special interests, the state's independent study has called for the continuation of the program. While an overall evaluation is still premature, the study has determined that the students are, at the very least, keeping strides with their public school peers - this from a group that had scored in the bottom third in national assessment measures while in the public schools. There is no question that the program enjoys strong parental support and involvement and has promoted better discipline, enthusiasm and attendance from the students.

Similar choice programs are thriving in more than 20 cities, including Milwaukee, with the benefit of private sponsors. From Los Angeles to San Antonio to Indianapolis, foundations like the Choice Charitable Trust and the Children's Educational Opportunity Foundation provide low-income families half-tuition scholarships to help them send their children to the school of their choice, whether

"[Brittany] is more eager to learn and more receptive to learning. The school offers a wide variety of subjects such as access to computers .... It is a lot more creative, the class size is smaller and she has exposure to older children which helps with the learning process and makes the work more challenging. In the public schools, on the other hand, there seems to be no focus on the individual child's needs, the classroom was overcrowded and the teachers seemed to hold a lot of resentment toward me when I tried to get involved and help my child. They had a lot of excuses why my child was not learning. It's really easy to get lost in the system. It's very frustrating and it's really a sad thing."

Single mother of choice student, Austin

"Katari has been in three schools in the past year in an effort to find a school that would work with him and his academic needs. It took some time for him to adjust to his new school, and he struggled with the new curriculum and environment at first, but his school has been able to give him the necessary encouragement and push for him to be able to pull his grades up. Now he is progressing better than he has in a long time."

Single mother of two, Milwaukee

"My granddaughter is considered dyslexic, and although she attended pre-kinder, kindergarten and three years of public school, there was very little done to help her [in her public school]. Her school work this year resembled work done by a first grader. She could not read or retain anything. She also had headaches, stomach aches, etc. and fought going to school. Other students teased her on grades and teachers claimed she had an attention difficulty, was lazy and did not turn in her school papers. No amount of consultations with teachers, counselors, principals or the San Antonio School Officer were of any help. Since she was considered dyslexic, they would not hold her back and instead kept promoting her. Then, a friend told us about [a school] that works with children having learning problems. [With your help] we enrolled her immediately and within 3 or 4 days her attitude was completely changed. She looks forward to going to school. Her writing is neat and clear. She now enjoys doing her homework. She has a long way to go, but we believe the stress has eased up."[22]

Grandmother of choice child, San Antonio

parochial, private or out-of-district public schools. Parents are required to pay their share, often half, of the school's tuition, but for the opportunity, they believe it's worth the sacrifice. As of September 1994, more than 8,500 children were using such scholarships, and at least as many children are on the waiting lists.[21] (The scholarships are awarded on a first come, first served basis - the only requirement is income level.) And schools are doing their part to foot the bill. Some have granted their own partial scholarships to help families make ends meet, and in Texas alone three new schools opened to accommodate children participating in these choice programs.

In 1994, Puerto Rico began its second year of offering the largest choice program that includes independent schools. Like the government program in Milwaukee and the independent programs there and in other cities, eligibility is determined by income level. While any child can transfer from one public school to another, tuition grants for independent schools are available only to the poor. More than 1,900 students from households with incomes below $18,000 attend independent schools under the commonwealth's choice program.[23] An even greater number of students - 14,922 - have used the choice program to attend public schools previously not opened to them.[24] Although the program has since been ruled unconstitutional, the complications were specific to Puerto Rican law and should have no effects on efforts stateside.

3: The Myths and Realities of School Reform

Good schools exist. And bad schools exist.

The challenge of school reform is to make all schools good schools. The only question is how best to do that.

Substantive, lasting reform is only going to come from a serious reevaluation of the ways in which today's schools operate. Systemic reform is not about reinventing the wheel or reinventing a system. It is about creating a climate that fosters innovation and provides an array of options within a community. To create that climate, you must understand more fully how schools operate.

Everyone has important questions about the schools and what is needed for improvement. Here you will find some of the most frequently asked questions followed by meaningful answers, not only to help you better understand the issues, but to help you explain them to others. In each case, more volumes can be and have been written. But whether you are trying to understand it yourself, or help someone else understand, it is important to keep it brief and straightforward.

Why all the talk about school reform?

Every parent and every teacher knows that different children benefit from different schools. Yet, despite the existence of over 15,000 separate school districts and nearly 85,000 individual public schools, by and large these schools have the same basic characteristics. And by and large they are all run the same - with an eye toward getting as many children through the twelve-grade process as possible, as easily as possible. Innovation is discouraged. Teachers are reduced to clock-punching factory workers, and students are simply cogs in the wheel. In an environment where failing students are simply passed up the grade ladder, students lose their incentive to excel. And parents report that they have no place in such a system at all. So, many people are demanding change.

Are things really as bad as they sound? My school is just fine.

There is countless evidence that, overall, even the best schools are not working to provide a real quality education. An October, 1994, *Money* magazine article underscores this fact. In its "report cards for seven types of schools," *Money* rates average public schools and disadvantaged public schools second to last and last, with overall grades of "C" and "D+" respectively.[1] That means that the majority of today's school children are attending "C" and "D+" - and failing - schools. They shouldn't have to.

Our community has a partnership that is seeking to change all that. Won't this take care of the problems?

Partnerships are fine, and they are necessary to building morale and awareness in any community. The best partnership, however, cannot fix a system that is by its very design flawed. More requirements have been placed on the schools to be all things to all people, regardless of what the

schools and the parents want. Schools are teaching things that many believe shouldn't be taught, and not teaching things that many believe should be taught. Discipline is virtually absent, and local business leaders report that they see far too many high school graduates who are functionally illiterate.

Meanwhile, bad policy has reinforced an unresponsive system, so that our best principals and teachers are limited in their ability to innovate or improve matters. And special interests are loathe to hand over any control over the system that will cut into their political powerbase. This is especially true of those aspects that govern hiring and firing or those that deal with setting academic standards. Thus community-student mentor programs, private donations for curriculum enrichment activities and other charitable work that make

Put Schools Before Rules

Boston, MA. There has been much talk of increasing the number of neighborhood, or "walk to," schools, often with the inference that busing and remaining court orders are the impediment [to good schools]. But only 36 percent of students choosing schools under the city's controlled choice program now ask to be assigned to their walk zone school. The obvious reason is that the education product isn't so good around the corner.

So the way to increase the use of neighborhood schools and reduce transportation costs is not to appeal to the court but to improve what is offered the students.[2]

up the bulk of partnerships, while well-intentioned, are not enough to undo a mess that has accumulated over time. They merely scratch the surface, rather than get to the core of the problems.

Aren't there ANY "good" schools?

In active, suburban communities you find some of the best schools in the country. Inner-city magnet schools that demand dedication on the part of administrators, teachers, parents and students achieve high results for their efforts. Charter schools that grow out of a community's need for and commitment to a different way of schooling excel. And independent, non-government schools of all stripes have consistently, traditionally, succeeded with every manner of student, including those at-risk.

Why do these schools work and yet so many of the public schools don't?

It's not more money, and it's not better kids. There are impoverished schools that shine and affluent schools that do not.

The effectiveness of a good school is largely the result of its parents, teachers and students who have control over their education process, and who every day exercise a choice to participate in and contribute to that process.

Consider charter schools. These are public schools that are self-governing and self-sustaining. They must meet their performance contract, and are free from most state regulations in order to do just that. Principals are the leaders in the charter school, and are ultimately responsible for their success and failure. Principals choose their own teams of teachers, who in turn are given latitude to govern their classrooms in the way they see fit. Finally, parents choose to send their children there, making an implicit contract between the parent and the school.

The Walt Whitman High School in suburban Bethesda, Maryland, is considered to be one of the finest in the Washington, D.C. area and, in fact, on the East Coast. But Whitman shares many of the same problems other less affluent schools have. One of its math teachers has reportedly urged his students to do their homework in class, while the teacher marks the previous day's homework. No questions to the teacher are allowed during that time. When parents of students who need more guidance than just the textbook inquire about this procedure, this "teacher" has responded, "hire a tutor."[3]

Effective schools share three main factors — school independence, high expectations and parental choice. Schools innovating to achieve these characteristics are making great strides.

What does choice in education mean?

When we talk about choice, we're talking about parents and students being able to choose the school that is right for them, instead of having to go to a school based on where they live. That means being able to pick the best school to suit your family's needs - a process much different than being assigned to the school that happens to be zoned to your neighborhood or having to move to qualify to send your children to the school you want.

When we talk about choice, we're also talking about teachers being able to choose where they teach, instead of being assigned by the district; teachers able to use their own creativity and motivation in their teaching, instead of being handed lesson plans by a steering committee. And we're talking about principals who can work to bring the best teachers to their school, instead of being stuck with uncommitted teachers the district had to put somewhere.

Choice requires commitment from parents, teachers, students and schools, and it leads to accountability for results. When parents and teachers can pick their schools, the schools will have to work hard to attract them. That means schools HAVE to be good to stay in business.

Does choice in and of itself make better schools?

Choice is a powerful catalyst for improvements in learning, teaching and management. Schools are funded on a per-pupil basis. In a choice environment, schools have a strong incentive to attract students and funding. Because parents, not bureaucrats, decide which school is best for their child, schools become responsive to parents. Existing schools are going to work harder to improve and excel, and new schools will be created to better meet the wide variety of families' and communities' needs. Schools will engage in a healthy competition to stay in business and to be the best. Schools that don't work will close and be replaced by schools that do.

Charters and magnet schools, for example, are tailor-made to deliver a unique, superior education. They would not exist without choice. Unlike

The more experience Peggy McGill had with the Milwaukee public education system, the more she dreamed of sending her sons to private school. She felt school was a violent place, not an educational haven. And when her children had trouble making good grades, no teacher ever called to talk about it.

McGill's final frustration came the day her younger son, Deshaun, complained that he was being bullied in the school yard every day at recess. When she confronted the school vice principal, she was told plainly: ''If you want to keep your son in this school, you must teach him to fight.'' Deshaun was only 6 years old.

"It got to the point where I couldn't take it anymore," said McGill, a single mother. But with her $20,000 salary as a computer operator for an insurance company, private school tuition was a luxury she could not afford.

Then friends told her about Milwaukee's new ''school choice'' program. The year was 1990, and Wisconsin lawmakers had just signed a law offering low-income children tax-financed vouchers for tuition at any participating private, nonreligious school in the city.

Upon hearing of Milwaukee's program, McGill immediately chose Harambee, a small school with an emphasis on Black history and cultural pride. Its Swahili name means ''coming together.'' Deshaun, now 9, and his older brother Tawaun, 14, have attended the private school at no charge and have worn its green-and-white uniform for three years.

''They're getting a real good education now, which I don't feel they would have gotten if they were in the public schools,'' McGill said.

''The vouchers have been helpful to us in trying to be racially, ethnically, economically and religiously diverse,'' said [Harambee] Principal Sue Wing. ''Before them, we had virtually no scholarship money available. Now we do.'' Parents are required to help with fund-raising and must show up at teacher conferences to receive their children's report cards, something the public schools may not require.

Shirley Bell, a single mother earning $10,000 a year as a nursing assistant, arrived at Woodlands [choice school] to pick up her two little girls, who skipped down the steps to greet her.

''I think everybody should have a choice of where to go to school,'' Bell said as she grasped each child's hand. "If they had better help in the public schools, we wouldn't be having this debate."[4]

Voni Eason is one D.C. parent who made the choice to switch her 5-year-old son, Veronza, from public to private school. The Washington Scholarship Fund, a nonprofit organization established this year, pays half her son's tuition at a local parochial school. "My child is a black male coming from a single-parent family headed by a female, so he has a few strikes against him just by being born," says Mrs. Eason. Young African-American males, in fact, are 9 times as likely to be the victims of homicide as white males, and almost twice as likely to drop out of school. But Mrs. Eason strongly believes that a good education can help her son buck the odds.

When Mrs. Eason found the public school teaching Veronza the same skills he had already learned in preschool, she pulled him out. "I did not like the education he was getting in the public school system. I need him to advance, not to review things he's already learned." She also grew alarmed at the public school's shift toward bilingual education. Mrs. Eason doesn't mind her son learning a second language, "but before you learn Spanish, you've got to learn English!"

Tanya Odemns is another parent who grew frustrated with the public schools. Her son struggled in school and began to act up in class after being repeatedly teased by classmates. She was told her son was a "problem child," requiring special education. For Miss Odemns, that was the last straw. When I heard about [the Washington Scholarship Fund], I just hopped on it real quick." Thanks to a voucher, Miss Odemns was able to enroll Vernon in the Naylor Road School in her neighborhood. "My son knows how to add, how to subtract. Whenever he sees words he knows, he wants to spell them. He's happy now."

Despite help from vouchers, paying the tuition balance can still extract a heavy toll from low-income families. The Smith family gets a hand sending its three children to Catholic schools from the Children's Education Foundation in Atlanta. To obtain an added tuition break, 15-year-old Billy works an hour a day in the school cafeteria. Billy's mother, Joy, volunteers mornings at the elementary school. And one Saturday a month, the whole family cleans the local church. But that still wasn't enough. Last year, Joy Smith and her husband gave up health insurance in order to keep their children in school. "We'd be so much better off financially if we put our children in public school, but this is our choice," explains Mrs. Smith. "We want our children to get a better education than we did so they can succeed in life," says Maria Chavez, trying to put the bankruptcy of the family's auto upholstery business behind her. "I didn't get a good enough education in the public school system to keep up with college. I got lost. I don't want that to happen to my kids," adds her husband, Antonio. The Chavezes pay about $110 a month to educate all three of their children at St. Mary Magdalene elementary school in San Antonio; the Children's Educational Opportunity (CEO) Foundation pays the other half of the tuition.[5]

regular public schools, no one can be forced to attend them, so they have to recruit students. (And teachers have to choose to teach there.) They have to keep those students coming back - if they do that, they keep their funding, and their doors stay open. If they don't, they're shut down.

Choice provides an opportunity for major improvements, such as the demonstrated rise in parental involvement and satisfaction in Milwaukee choice program or the reinvestment of actual *surpluses* in some California charter schools. In Minnesota, public schools increased advanced-placement class offerings in order to compete with the enrollment options provided by local colleges. Innovative charter schools for at-risk youth graduate former dropouts, and are attracting mainstream students interested in the success of smaller schools. Public schools, in return, design "schools within schools" focusing on everything from environmental science to business and leadership to performing arts, all in order to persuade students to stay. They all must work to improve.

Are there examples of where school choice is working?

The exciting news is that there are a variety of examples in action: in the 15 states and over 100 school districts that have invited - in some cases required - parents to decide which school is right for their child; between districts, within entire states, and even across a few state lines; in the hundreds more magnets, charters and schools-within-schools, where parents line up to register days in advance and some children travel across town to take advantage of a better education; and, finally, in the 20 parental choice grant programs that provide parents with financial assistance, giving them more choices in picking the right school for their child.

These reforms all sound well and good, but what about making all schools good schools?

This is a statement most often made by the representatives of the various education groups. It is disarming to most of us because we all want all schools to be good. Translated, however, the question means that shouldn't we add money to all schools so that they all can be as good as the next? In fact, were that the answer, all schools would have been great long ago. A decade of research tells us that more of everything - whether it is money, graduation requirements, teachers or technology - doesn't bring any reform

Model Schools within Schools

One school in New York achieved so much success with the school-within-a-school for gifted students that it's expanding the concept to the whole school. South Shore High School in Rockaway beach is "splitting their collection of four-story buildings into six distinct schools with separate faculties, curricula and traditions."

"We have come to the conclusion that schools of 3,000 are no good any more," said South Shores principal Rina Stempel. "We want to give the rest of the kids a sense of community like the scholars have."

The move is in keeping with a big new idea in American education: smaller is better. Ever since innovators like East Harlem's Deborah Meier showed in the 1980s that large urban schools could work better if broken into pieces, educators across the country have been looking for ways to split their largest and most difficult high schools.

Philadelphia's charter school movement is designed to give high school students smaller, cozier environments and more frequent contact with small groups of teachers. California's vocational academies rely on their small size as well as their career focus to keep students involved in school. A handful of other states are running similar programs.

Nearly every study of urban high school dropouts has shown that students stay in school when a teacher or administrator shows a regular interest in them and leave when they fail to establish such a relationship.[6]

if the actual character of the school is not changed.

Don't the schools need more money?

Make no mistake, money is critical to any institution's survival. Much of what is spent today, however, is squandered throughout the bureaucracy. In some cities less than 33 cents of every dollar is spent for kids in the classroom. And even pouring money directly into the classrooms - through reduced class sizes, higher teacher pay and more programs - does not automatically make for a good school. Research indicates that there is no correlation between money and achievement in a bad system. Many effective schools are, in fact, impoverished - lack of funds should not be allowed as an excuse for poor schools. With the right ingredients any school can be good, and good schools are more likely to be rewarded with more money by happy customers through their votes on school budgets and the like.

I support our current system because it is democratic, promising free access to all kids. Won't choice lead to exclusionary, segregated schools?

Sadly, many public schools, especially those in the inner cities, are more segregated today than 40 years ago when Brown v. Board of Education declared racially segregated schools illegal. The pressure for school reform has been greatest in areas where children are forced to attend substandard schools, particularly in the inner-cities. For these children, who live in disadvantaged circumstances, education is supposed to be the leg up to a better future. But what if their district-assigned school is overrun with discipline and safety problems, or their principal is powerless to make important employment decisions; what if children have been left behind in special-education classes based on their ethnic backgrounds? Such kids have been abandoned by the system that was supposed to help them.

But for kids who have a choice, they have a chance. Choice has been used successfully in cities like Boston, Massachusetts, New Haven, Connecticut, and Montclair, New Jersey, to spur voluntary racial integration. Requiring schools to attract students by choice, has forced schools to become better. Integration follows good education - anywhere.

Many existing charter schools were created to respond to failures in the local public school. A charter school in an Hispanic neighborhood in California caters to bilingual youth who were not getting adequate support in their public school. Most charter school laws actually require that a certain percentage of the new schools cater to disadvantaged children. And when school boards contract for educational services, many bring in private organizations to work with the most difficult students and the most poorly performing schools. For example, districts in seven states contract with Ombudsman Education Services, a private company, to give a second chance to students on the verge of dropping out.

In 1993, more than two dozen teachers at Webb Elementary School in Northeast Washington, D.C., walked out to protest the poor heating of their school building. Although steps had been taken to fix the school's two boilers, they still were not operating properly, spurring the teachers' protests.

The opening of the 1994-95 Washington, D.C., school year was delayed several days due to rampant fire code violations in many school buildings. After a parents advocacy group filed suit, a superior court judge found that the 160-plus schools had over 2,600 major "life-threatening" violations. The District paid nearly $8 million in labor and supplies to get the rush job done in time for the new school year. Maintenance workers worked around the clock to repair and replace broken doors and sprinkler systems to bring the schools up to code.[7]

All this despite spending more than $9,000 per child to run the schools in the nation's capital.

I've heard quite a bit about why school choice *won't* work, and frankly, it makes a lot of sense.

Faced with the increasing pressure from communities for real systemic education reform, the growing number of elected officials supporting those reforms and the on-going documentation of the success of such reforms, opponents are fighting hard to keep control. To do so they've launched an unprecedented misinformation campaign on school reform. They shamelessly create and perpetuate myths designed to obscure the facts and alarm and attack citizens who just want to improve the schools for the children.

> In the San Francisco public school system, 20% of the student body is black, but 50% of students assigned to special education programs are black. "Classes for the gifted usually mean classes for the white, and special education classes usually mean classes for black males," according to Federal Judge Robert L. Carter, the NAACP lawyer who argued Brown v. Board of Education. Furthermore, says the judge, "More black children are in all or virtually all black schools today than in 1954."[8]

What kind of myths do opponents perpetuate?

Opponents charge that today's parents don't care about making an informed choice about where their child goes to school, or that parents, particularly those in disadvantaged circumstances, are *UNABLE* to make a good decision for their child. As a result, such opponents contend, school choice will funnel all the best students from the best families into the best schools, and leave the worst students behind in the lousiest schools. To their credit, at least they're admitting that lousy schools exist and that any child forced to attend such a school has indeed been abandoned by the public school system.

In fact, poor, uneducated and otherwise disadvantaged parents, when given even the barest opportunity to affect the education their children receive, leap at the chance. The parents of over 8,500 students, all living below the poverty line, are taking advantage of privately funded parental choice scholarships to send their child to the school of their choice - be it an independent school or a public school for which they don't geographically qualify.

It seems like these choice schools are fueled by responsible and involved parents — what happens to the kids that don't have that benefit?

Regis Chesir, is an eighth-grader who entered The Urban Day School in Milwaukee as a "totally irresponsible" kid who never finished his homework. Now he has a solid B average and is the captain of the basketball team.

Gloria Collins enrolled her daughter, Natasha, in Urban Day because she could not read nor do simple arithmetic and had to be forced to go to school. Now, [3 years later] in the sixth grade, she is earning a steady C average.

More important to Collins, a dropout who got her high school equivalency degree and works as a teacher's assistant at Urban Day, Natasha is happy about going to school each morning. Collins says her daughter's positive attitude is all the proof she needs that choice is a success. "In public schools if you don't have it, they won't work with you to get it," she said. "They let you ride along until you get fed up with riding and you drop out." Every parent is expected to be involved in the school. Urban Day's motto this year is: "It takes a whole village to raise a child." Discipline is tough, but the atmosphere is warm.

Principal Robb Rauh took a 50% pay cut from his California teaching job to come to Urban Day as a teacher in 1990, the year the program was introduced. In classroom after classroom in the impeccably clean, colorfully decorated school, students are well-behaved and engaged in their work. The test results do not reflect it yet, but Rauh believes they soon will show the school is having a positive impact on students' academic abilities. "The people who live in the immediate neighborhood did not have a lot of choice before," he said.

"I never had a teacher that I felt cared about me and wanted to help me until I came to Harambee," said fourth-grader Ethan Hill, dressed in one of Harambee's forest green-and-white uniforms. [Half of Harambee's 420 students are choice students.] "Too many eighth-graders were picking on me because I got good grades," Elton Gofoe, 9, added. "Here, good grades are cool."

Ruthie Brown, Harambee's full-time disciplinarian, says choice provides a glimmer of hope for the children who live in its rough, gang-run neighborhood, where drive-by shootings and drugs are part of daily life. Harambee does not tolerate bad behavior; children who are sent to Brown's basement office are told to drop to the floor and do push-ups before getting on with the work their classmates are doing upstairs. But she doesn't send children back to class without letting them know she cares about them.

"I'm doing this to save our children," said Brown, who lives in the neighborhood and has sent her children to Harambee. "We've got a lost generation out there, and we're going to lose another one unless we help them develop self-discipline and self-esteem and provide a safe place for them to learn."[9]

With the introduction of public school choice in Los Angeles and Orange Counties, parents began looking at and finding out about their schools at a whole new level. "Parents are buzzing: Finally, they can enroll their children anywhere in the system regardless of where they live ... [Parents are] interviewing principals, attending classes and orientation meetings, and collecting test scores. Even parents who were considering private schools are rethinking their options."

"Parents in some Orange County school districts also have been busy discussing how parental choice may change their schools .... 'We've had some choices before, but not this wide open. People like this.'"[10]

Good choice programs have well-designed parental information centers and actively encourage outreach to the community. Schools that have to compete for students will automatically have to reach out to let parents know what they offer their students. For example, when open enrollment was introduced in Los Angeles in 1993, schools mobilized to get the word out to parents, inviting them to visit during the school day and even encouraging them to hop a school bus to get there. Such sharing of information and competing for students will make all the schools work harder, and if all schools improve, all children benefit.

But isn't all this really just about getting rid of public schools?

Opponents contend that school choice will cause children to flee from the majority of existing public schools and rush to charters, magnets and private schools. This argument, of course, is a confession of public school failings - but it's not how choice works. Schools should be closed down if they will not work to improve, but the evidence suggests that most schools improve in response to the fact that their livelihood now depends upon consumer choice. The point of choice is to improve and expand public education so that many different types of education are possible and encouraged. Contrary to one of opponents' noisiest contentions, when folks do have a choice, they don't necessarily opt for a private school. They just want to find the best possible education for their child. For example, in 1994, the second year of Puerto Rico's choice program, of the 17,000 students who chose a different school, a majority chose a different public school and less than a quarter went from public to private.[11]

These claims of a conspiracy against public schooling would be laughable if they weren't so often put forth by the education establishment in earnest. In reality, there would be no exodus of children - there would be,

The Milwaukee Parental Choice Program provides tuition assistance to children from low-income families to attend alternative schools to the Milwaukee public schools. In 1993-1994, 733 students participated. These students were achieving at the bottom third coming out of their public school, compared to students nationwide. 60% of the families earned less than $10,000 a year. Over 70% of the choice students were African-American; 20% were Hispanic.

Says Democratic Assemblywoman Polly Williams of the program she pushed through the legislature, "The issue is very simple. It is a good program, the kids are learning, leave them alone. The parents are saying that they are not going to tolerate their children being miseducated anymore and that they are the ones who are ultimately responsible for what happens to their children."

"I am one of those people who is supposed to be very stupid because I am black, I live in the inner city, I am poor, and I raised my children in a single parent home. Well, those are lies. The only thing different about us is that we have been deprived of resources and access. When you empower parents like me, there is a major difference. We become responsible for our own lives. We want to be empowered, and that is what the choice program has done.[12]

however, an exodus of special interests who would no longer be in control of our schools.

Aren't these sorts of reforms really just a pet issue of the ultra conservatives and "the radical right"?

Actually, school choice, charters and other efforts enjoy a very diverse base of support. Of the reforms enacted into law, a majority was pushed through by Democrats. Similarly, of the state and local leaders working for more reforms, support comes equally from African-American, Hispanic and Anglo individuals and communities.

Well, issues like choice don't apply to my situation. We live in a rural area with few schools.

Choice can be defined in many ways. Rural areas can easily free their schools from rules and regulations and offer choice to teachers to decide what kinds of programs they'd like to teach and possibly design. Charter schools provide a unique solution to the problems of rural schools because they are adaptable to the specific needs of a small community, and they don't need to fit the traditional school-house mold. Likewise, a system of choice may allow new schools to situate in your rural school district. Or, as Minnesota has found, schools-within-schools - separate and distinct programs operating out of the same building - can work wonders in providing more choices and autonomy. In New York's East Harlem, teachers created over 50 new "schools" in only 20 buildings, and such setups can work equally well in rural areas.

"Too often the educational system has failed our children ... too often it even frustrates the teachers themselves, making it hard for them to respond well to the needs of our children. Even worse, some schools, some administrators, and some teachers are not sensitive to our culture, our language, and our values. This makes it harder for our children to learn. It causes too many to drop out of school. And it makes it harder for parents to help their children learn and get a good education.

"Open enrollment, charter schools, parental choice grants, teacher training, and special programs for at-risk students can help parents have real choices. Today we announce our support for education reform that can help parents obtain better education for their children.

"The Arizona Hispanic Community Forum, together with Chicanos Por La Causa, Valle Del Sol, other Latino organizations, parents and many community members, ask the legislature to put aside the concerns of special interests and pass legislation that will move this society toward meaningful educational reform. We all owe our children no less."

Arizona Hispanic Community Forum,
February 15, 1994

But if regulations are waived for these schools won't that lead to unsafe, irresponsible schools?

Discrimination, safety and health laws apply to *all* schools. Just as all existing choice programs emphasize enforcement of anti-discrimination laws, all charters are tied to performance contracts detailing student achievement levels, which are revoked if the terms are not met. In addition, we must remember that nothing prevents unsafe, irresponsible schools from opening and attracting customers today.

Regulation waivers don't apply to laws governing safety, health and basic civil rights. Instead, only certain regulations are waived - those interfering with local school decisions. Stifling regulations disappear, and basic regulations required of any school, public or private, are left in place. The remaining guidelines do not interfere with content, but ensure that what is advertised is provided. For example, most states insist *all* schools meet minimum academic standards.

Right now, public schools spend too much time and money complying with thousands of mandates that have no bearing on the education of children. In New York, some poorly performing schools file extra reports to justify how they spend their money. But explaining away the spending is not a substitute for explaining why children aren't receiving a good education. When schools have to answer directly to parents and taxpayers for academic results, instead of merely reporting to bureaucrats on a thousand details of how they run their day, they'll have to be responsible. Thousands of district and independent schools already do, and are delivering a top-notch education.

What about private organizations working with the public schools - won't kids' education take a back seat to making a buck?

Private businesses have more incentive to make schools work because their livelihoods depend on it. They don't make any money unless they deliver a good product. Parents and students must want to participate in their programs. These entrepreneurs are bound also by performance contracts that spell out just how well they must do. If they don't measure up, the school district can close them down on short notice.

Rank and file teachers realize the opportunities that school reform will give them and students. They are sometimes the most effective champions of new approaches, despite their affiliation with unions opposed to change. In an electronic conversation, one National Education Association (NEA) member asserted, "We need to decide if [public schools] are the buildings or the concepts. If the concept - everyone helping through taxes to educate all the children - then we can do education in lots of different places." Said another, in support of California charter schools, "One charter school is an attempt to rid itself of a totally inept board. I hope that the hundred charter schools allowed will provide some fresh direction for our fine school system."

Can't the public schools change without this stuff?

The present day system offers no incentives to change. In the inertia of the public school system, schools open and shut based on the rise and fall in local population. A failing school stays open year after year in a crowded neighborhood. Poor or unmotivated teachers teach there year after year with no incentive to improve and no mechanism for dismissal, while good teachers lose their enthusiasm. And, there is little room for real parental involvement, resulting in a poor relationship between parents and teachers.

Schools of choice can provide more freedom to teachers, require administrators to be more efficient and better managers, and encourage higher standards for children.

These questions only touch on some of the concerns so often voiced about systemic school reform, and new myths spring up just as old ones are finally put to rest. But much literature exists to combat these myths, to expand your understanding of school reform, and to inform you about the new and good things taking place in schools across the country. For an in-depth look at various issues and information about programs, see our appendices for further reading and resource contacts.

Who's in Charge: The Education Establishment

4: Who's In Charge? An Overview.

Education is an industry. Like most major industries that grew out of the industrial revolution, it has its factory workers and their unions, its managers, its special interests and consumers. Over time, a productive business, whether the local bank or a large national corporation, downsizes to stay afloat. Not so with education. Education is bigger than ever. It has lost its friendliness and ability to respond. It has grown out-of-control; not because consumer satisfaction has allowed it to, but because of laws and regulations that stop schools from working.

Since 1945, the number of school districts has been consolidated from over 100,000 to just 15,173 school districts in 1992. Instead of locally run, the public school system has become more and more centralized, with power in the bureaucracy, not the community. State and federal education dollars carry layers of regulation and conditions. For example, the California State Education Code is over 6,000 pages long.[1] In Indiana, a much smaller state, all state education codes amount to 1,250 pages. In the first half of 1994, the federal government passed nine new laws mandating how dollars are spent and how schooling should occur.

How did this happen? How did the business of schooling get so out of hand? The American tradition of schooling rests with the states, where it is delegated to individual communities. State Boards of Education and legislators are supposed to set the broad goals, and those closest to our children are supposed to decide and carry out what really happens. But as the layers of bureaucracy have increased, parents have been able less and less to make a dent in their schools in any basic way. Yes, a parent can volunteer in a classroom or library in some cases. And, she can probably help the teacher design a plan for her child's progress through history class - sometimes. At one time, that parent could have influenced the character of the school - its teaching methods, curriculum, and special programming - through her votes for the school board. Things are no longer that easy.

Why They Call it "The Blob"

Parents say they have little power to affect good things in their schools. They feel that no matter where they turn, they cannot get through the maze of bureaucratic rules. In some cases, even school personnel can be hostile to their concerns. And with the government dictating what they do, the schools are powerless to respond and build real partnerships with parents. Much of this has happened by sheer momentum. Much has been caused also by the very groups whose stated mission is to "better" our

A View on Waste

I went from being a businessman to being a teacher and later a school administrator .... My first hard lesson was to try to fire an incompetent, disinterested, unwilling teacher. His lawsuit, filed to contest the dismissal, took 10 months. His fellow teachers who had snickered about the teacher's "distraction" before now testified in his defense, even though they knew little about what went on in his classroom. This district and I lost the suit. The teacher was reinstated.

When I was transferred to another school, I found that teachers refused to chaperon dances. We couldn't find coaches for the teams, and teachers were racing the kids out of the parking lot at 3:15. Since then, the teachers have negotiated a maximum of 275 minutes instructional time per day (4 hours, 35 minutes), 180 days a year. They get extra pay for any extra activities, and they may leave the school site at the end of the instructional day, which is now 2:30. Their average pay is now $52,127 per year for working less than 66% of a corporate work year.

As buildings and grounds administrator, I oversaw part of the budget. It cost $140,000 to maintain the swimming pool. I was surprised that while we paid for this, we could not buy the English department textbooks, even though they were using 8-year-old texts and didn't have enough to send one home with each student.

The schools have had 10 years to reform since "A Nation At Risk" was published. The years' growth in the union's power, "sweetheart" labor contracts, intimidating law suits, bureaucratic growth, and the inertia of a massive system have all worked against positive change. The schools are now much worse! The chaotic public school classrooms of the inner cities are beyond belief. The expensive non-performance in all public schools is inexcusable.[2]

schools. These groups are the education establishment — the blob. As a testament to their position, the National Education Association (NEA) president boasted to his board of directors in 1993: "NEA had unprecedented input into several key education issues including education reform legislation ... NEA also played a major role as President Clinton began forming his cabinet and senior staff. NEA was directly involved in helping to build the best team possible for the U.S. Department of Education."

Including the NEA, the education establishment has over 200 groups with a vested interest in a particular aspect of the education industry. From the National Alliance of Business to the National School Public Relations Administrators, the blob now runs the schools because it is so influential in politics - both in school board races and lobbying state leaders and Washington. They have the money, the power and have been a political fixture for years. They not only have secured a safe haven for their own agenda but have severely limited the ability of individual communities to maintain input, much less control, over the schooling their children receive.

At the local level, parents are often paid lip service, and parents who ask a lot of questions are considered troublemakers. Administrators are now accountable to other administrators, not to the people. Parental involvement is often just window dressing. When a complaint or suggestion is voiced that is not consistent with the views of the education establishment, the parents are branded as "difficult" or worse. This has set up a situation that frustrates even the most enthusiastic supporters of public education.

The picture is bleak. Even the best spirit of cooperation in the most unified community will yield few results if those active in that community do not know the right questions to ask and what the obstacles are. As people's satisfaction with their schools has declined, the groups claiming to defend the schools cling tighter to the status quo and lobby harder and louder for more of those programs - many non-education in scope - that will protect their position. Sadly, the rank and file of any of these education groups are helpless to do anything about it. Teachers, the most important people in our schools, next to our children, have been left out in the cold.

In the next chapters we explain what the organizations are that represent different aspects of the schools and what you can do to work within - or outside - of these structures.

5: The Unions

Unions were begun as professional associations to provide benefits support to teachers. Today, they are the most powerful and pervasive block of influence in the schools. Rather than being a positive voice for all matters of schooling, they are obsessed with control over all employment policies. No district can operate without their approval of contracts, and principals only have whatever authority a contract for the whole district gives them to hire, fire and reward - virtually none at all. The unions claim to promote teacher professionalism, yet crusade against salary and merit rewards for teachers. The unions have forced rules on the system that make it difficult for a school to dismiss someone for incompetence, or even misconduct. The unions believe the only requirement to become a teacher should be an "approved" teaching degree, regardless of one's competence in a particular subject.

Today's teachers unions are no longer concerned with just employee benefits issues. Through their collective bargaining power, the unions maintain de facto control of budgetary and management issues that appear beyond their influence and are thought to be controlled by school boards and administrators. In Boston, for example, even the slightest changes in the length of the school year could not be made without changing the union's contract. From hiring and firing to curriculum, and from money to testing, the teachers unions wield incredible power over how and by whom the schools are run. And that's just for starters.

The National Education Association (NEA) is not only the largest teachers union in the country, but the largest labor union in the world, period. At over 2.2 million members, it is nearly three times as large as the 850,000-member American Federation of Teachers (AFT). Together these two teachers unions create a network of influence that reaches into every state, city and school district in the nation. Nearly 70 percent of the nation's public school teachers are members of either the NEA or the AFT.[1] Both groups are highly organized, highly active national political organizations that can muster unprecedented grass roots access - neither the Republican nor the Democratic national party can compare in political muscle. Boasts the NEA, "We are the only organization in the United States with a nation-

This is the story of a convicted felon in the education system. A New York City teacher was arrested for selling drugs in May of 1989. Under tenure rules, he was moved to an administrative position, for which he continued to be paid, even after he pleaded guilty to felony drug charges and began to serve a prison sentence. His teacher status got him into the work-release program, and by the next fall, he was back at his administrative job. It was not until two years later that the Board of Education got around to dismissing him. But, it didn't end there. The Education Commissioner later changed the dismissal to a two year suspension without pay, and in May, 1994, the teacher began negotiations with the board for a fall *teaching* position. The Board of Education spent more than five years and $185,000 on this one teacher's disciplinary proceedings.

The New York State School Board Association reports that school districts in New York spend, on average, about 18 months and $194,000 (including the teacher's salary and that of the substitute) to prosecute every such case. A spokesman for the New Jersey School Boards Association said that state spends about $100,000 and one year to adjudicate each case.

As of June, 1994, the New York board's Office of Legal Services was processing cases involving 158 teachers and 18 other tenured educators on charges ranging from sex crimes to chronic absence. "An arts teacher has been charged with helping an immigrant student run away from home by harboring her in his apartment. A principal has been charged with stealing $10,000 in school funds. A gym teacher has been charged with having sex with a teen-age girl in the school weight room. Though all have been transferred to administrative posts, they continue to draw full salaries." In the last five years, the board has only dismissed 28 tenured teachers.

"Some defense lawyers intentionally drag cases out because their clients enjoy administrative reassignment. In one case a Brooklyn teacher reassigned in 1991 for hitting students acknowledged that he preferred his temporary job over classroom duties. After he was cleared on one charge, he struck another student, and a panel concluded that he had engineered the incident in order to return to a desk job."[2]

wide, broad-based pool of education advocates in every precinct."[3] Nearly one of every eight delegates at the 1992 Democratic National Convention was an NEA member.

The national, state and local education associations work in concert, with little variety in their issues or agendas. The NEA is at work in the very heart of each community. The local union affiliate can sway the community with well-organized and well-funded opposition to reform. When they perceive a threat, the state organizations will charge members extra dues for their politicking. California teachers were assessed $63 each to help pay for the campaign against school choice Proposition 174.[4] The Michigan Education Association, in its fight against school reform legislation passed in December 1993, assessed its members $90 each and enlisted two teachers from each district, in addition to its 11 full-time lobbyists, to lobby state legislators against the bill.[5] At its July, 1994, annual convention it took the NEA only three and a half days to raise half a million dollars for its Political Action Committee from less than 10,000 delegates.

It is important to understand just how removed the NEA is from the interests of the people. The national network is organized out of the Washington, D.C., headquarters where hundreds of staffers coordinate state and local affairs. Its staff is visible in the halls of Congress and in state capitals. Its driving motivation has always been more money: the NEA says it wants no less than 10% of the federal budget to go for education. It says schools are underfunded and teachers are underpaid, but the agenda is not limited to helping teachers get paid more. Communities want their good teachers paid well and they are in some cases, regardless of the NEA. What the NEA demands is more money for programs that it - "the experts" - thinks are good, but that are often at odds with what a community wants or needs. Promoting pro-grams from bilingual education to gender equity, the NEA has successfully manipulated your tax dollars with no regard for whether these programs work.

Union Info

The Pennsylvania State Education Association pays out more than $15 million in salaries and benefits to its 250 employees - an average of $60,000 per staff member. During the 1993-94 year PSEA, the state's largest teachers union, employed nine registered lobbyists at a cost of $850,000. In 1992, the union's PAC spent over a half million dollars in campaign contributions. Despite this cash flow, the agenda of the PSEA has been frustrated in the Capitol; according to PSEA President Annette Palutis, the word is getting out "that public schools are failing ... and that we, as a union, are to blame. Those who have supported us in the past are finding it more difficult to support us and those who have not supported us in the past are stepping up the attack."[6]

Every year at its summer convention, NEA delegates vote on what to do about everything from the environment to abortion to foreign policy. The NEA "congressional contact team" interviews and monitors both candidates and elected officials to measure how well they meet NEA criteria on issues ranging from health care to civil rights. The NEA boasts of its power

At the NEA Conference

The 1994 National Education Association's annual convention theme was "Public Education is a Public Trust." President Keith Geiger in his opening address noted, "The NEA is in the forefront of political change ... at a time when public education and our Association are under relentless attack, we continue to grow. Since our last [annual meeting] we have added 37,663 members - which is equivalent to adding an entirely new Kentucky Education Association to our ranks in a single year! The NEA family today stands as the largest, most influential, most effective child advocacy organization on this planet."

Press releases indicated that issues to be discussed would include: privatization; integrating special education and medically fragile students into regular classrooms (also know as "inclusion"); health care; safe schools; education funding; and school accountability.

Other issues that the 10,000 union delegates chose to discuss at length included: U.S. foreign policy and human rights in Cuba, Serbia, Haiti and Rwanda; commemorative postage stamps; product boycotts; and NEA intervention on behalf of two individuals currently in American prisons.

The NEA bestowed its annual "Friend of Education Award" on David Berliner of Arizona State University. He spoke to the delegates on the state of today's public schools, which he called "a manufactured crisis." He made other noteworthy remarks throughout his half-hour speech. He claimed that:

◆ "the crises of contemporary American education were manufactured by people with an agenda that includes the destruction of public education as we know it."

◆ National Assessment of Educational Progress (NAEP) tests are "purposely designed to give the impression that we have no high achieving students;"

◆ U.S. Presidents and Secretary of Education have lied about how much the United States spends on education compared to other nations;

◆ "the worst thing that ever happened to education is the radio talk show."

He concluded that "school reform is nice, but community and family rebuilding is a much better, long-range strategy ... to give us the children we most want to teach."

Over the course of the convention, the NEA approved $1.6 million in spending to battle local school choice and private contracting measures and to "ward off conservative critics." An additional $1.5 million was added to its contingency fund to support state-level fights against choice.

to affect elections and, in most states, union leaders serve in elected or appointed positions, including local and state boards of education, as well as advisory committee posts.

The other teachers union, the American Federation of Teachers, is headed by Albert Shanker. Working with approximately 850,000 members, Shanker is somewhat more visionary than most, and he is someone who can be just as often for good reforms as against them. His independence also makes the affiliates a little more independent, but they still generally flex their muscles by fighting reforms that upset the current power structure.

Someday we may not have to differentiate between the two largest teacher unions, because there is interest in a merger. Together, the resulting union would be more than twice as big as the next largest labor organization in the country. Formed in the name of "consistency" in organization and direction, the new behemoth would surely continue to support the status quo. That is why it is important for states and communities to take back their schools now.

The political dynamics have begun to change. In 1994, nearly all the newly elected state governors were not endorsed by the NEA and its allies. The composition of many state legislatures changed to reflect less union-dictated views, and as a result of several U.S. Senate races, the NEA lost ground.

There is further evidence that the NEA's power is waning. Even candidates who were targeted by the NEA for defeat for their views on school reform have won at the ballot box. The NEA's $500,000 allocation at its annual conference aimed at defeating reform Governor John Engler of Michigan failed to have any impact. Arizona's State Superintendent of Schools, Lisa Graham, was opposed by the union but won her race handily. And the Idaho Education Association readily admit-

The National Teacher's Examination (NTE) is a test that is usually required before a prospective teacher candidate can receive a credential to teach in the schools. Most believe this exam helps determine a person's qualifications for the job. The following question appeared in 1993 on the exam and is not unique for the NTE: "What is the role of a teachers union in public schools?" One wonders what this has to do with whether a person is qualified to teach English or math. The Educational Testing Service administers the NTE and relies heavily on the input of people within the education establishment for direction. Obviously, that question was written by someone who felt it was critical information for evaluating future teachers.

ted that "it took a beating" when Dr. Anne Fox became Idaho's new superintendent. While beatable, however, the NEA is no weak opponent.

Who's In Charge:

The NEA and the AFT are national organizations, and their affiliates are in control throughout the states. Baltimore, Maryland and New York state, for instance, are mostly under the AFT umbrella, while California and Minnesota are mostly NEA. There are other state and local teacher organizations that don't affiliate with either of the big two, such as the Missouri State Teachers Association and the Mississippi Professional Educators, but these are the exceptions to the rule.

What You Can Do:

The teachers unions do not necessarily represent the will of individual teachers, even if they belong to their local union. Be on the lookout for individual teachers who may want to help and are proponents of real reform. A public school teacher who will openly support your position brings credibility and an air of non-partisanship and fairness to your organization. But, be understanding of the fact that a teacher willing to do so may be taking both professional and personal risks.

6: The District

I. District School Boards and Superintendents

School districts are the only place most people will ever see the education process at work. They are made up of components that most of us are familiar with: the school board, superintendents and staff, principals and teachers. Most school boards are elected, although three percent - mostly in big cities - are appointed by city councils or mayors. School boards are traditionally responsible for running the show; they review and approve budgets, help set broad policy and other program issues. Generally, the superintendent must confer with his school board before he can make any organizational or contractual changes, such as establishing magnet schools or contracting out for food or transportation services with a private company.

There are exceptions. The superintendent in New York City's District 4, the East Harlem example mentioned earlier, implemented a school choice and local management program without approval by the district's governing board. He reasoned that the bureaucracy would take so long to catch up with him that, by that time, his new choice program would already be underway and working. It was - and is.

The school board *should* have full authority over the local public schools. However, that authority is so splintered among various office holders and special interests that its power is greatly diminished. On one hand, local school boards find their hands tied by thousands of regulations against making significant changes or even contributions to the running of the school district. On the other hand, winners of school board elections or

Most states authorize school districts to contract only with other government entities for instructional services. A number of state boards of education, however, are empowered to contract with private organizations to provide education and other services. States that allow such contracting in one form or another include: Arizona, California, Colorado, Connecticut, Delaware, Georgia, Idaho, Indiana, Iowa, Maryland, Minnesota, Nebraska, New Mexico, North Carolina, Ohio, Oregon, Utah, Vermont, Washington, Wisconsin. This contracting includes everything from sending children with behavior problems to private schools to using commercial companies to teach languages.

American Association of Educators in Private Practice Survey of States, Spring 1994

appointments are often those who have the blessing of the education establishment. So, the boards are no longer civil servants of the community but a power in their own right.

As the primary governing body of the district's schools, it is the school board that will most often challenge the unions. Often, the administrators and school board associations will be at odds with the unions. As a result, the unions put a lot of effort and money into electing their people onto school boards. Teachers unions take advantage of typical low turnouts for school board elections as "a better way to achieve their goals than striking." They get sympathizers onto the local governing bodies and try to control both the management and labor sides of the bargaining table.[3] An election in the Deer Valley School District in Phoenix, Arizona, is a good example. Between the two candidates vying for an open seat on the school's governing board, one was a longtime resident and supporter of the state's charter school law; the other candidate had only moved into the district a year previous and was an active union member. For this tiny election, nevertheless, the union spent $15,000 to seat its candidate, versus $500 spent by the reform candidate; the union candidate won. In 1993, the NEA's Center for the Preservation of Public Education spent $50,000 to combat school board candidates whose views did not match their own.[4] As a result, teachers unions often have greater influence over school board officials than the general public does.

In obtaining control of the school boards, unions gain access to school decisions at every level. Here they influence finances, since boards are in charge of setting school budgets. Communities vote on these budgets in most

At The School Boards Conference

The 1994 annual conference of the National School Boards Association covered such topics as: political skills, personal liability, media relations and free trade.[1] Some of the most highly attended seminars discussed Outcome Based Education and the Religious Right. At a seminar on the status of school choice, one speaker acknowledged that "Public education needs to be developing [alternative] choice plans because it's coming," to enthusiastic applause.

Most school board members at the conference were primarily concerned with protecting their control over the district from interference from the likes of outspoken *parents* and charter school proponents. But, they were also concerned with making sure they got as much money as possible from federal sources, thus actually inviting more oversight, not less. Rather than discuss issues such as how well our kids know their history, board members were preoccupied with how to get more money and how to get rid of bothersome parents and independent superintendents.[2]

places, but the process is often only a rubber stamp. For example, school boards have the authority to propose tax changes. However, in some instances a community's 'no' vote against new taxes will still result in increases. This is because states, like New York, then require school boards to enforce new budgets which are set as identical to the previous year's, plus an *increase* to cover inflation. Or, boards threaten cuts to "non-essential" programs for the children, like sports, rather than cutting administrative costs. Then, citizens committed to their sports programs immediately feel forced to vote for the inflated budget in an effort to save such options, even though they're in favor of the schools' trimming down.

The people do vote, but their power is often limited to marginal issues or a choice between the lesser of two evils. And in some states, even that level of input is threatened. In 1994, states such as Missouri, Montana and Oregon tried to give exclusive authority to the public to decide tax rates but were defeated through establishment opposition.[6]

School boards have shown some creativity in budget matters. They have discovered that the private sector often provides more service for the money. By contracting out to the private sector for everything from busing to food services to maintenance, districts have saved hundreds of thousands of dollars while receiving a more cost-efficient, superior delivery of services.

School boards can make big differences in states with charter schools. In many cases, they must approve charter proposals first. Some boards are hostile to charter schools because they are not controlled by school

School boards are often very political and try to please everyone, avoiding unpopular actions at all cost. William Bainbridge, the president and CEO of the Ohio-based School Match Company, says that "Boards of Education have been known to press administrators to take on 'dirty jobs,' such as closing schools or dismissing entrenched personnel. Many superintendents and former superintendents have interesting stories to tell regarding the board's negative reaction when complaints are lodged as a result of such board-directed actions." Boards also can put administrators in awkward negotiating positions with the unions. They are frequently sent into bargaining sessions with teacher groups encouraged to "hold the line" on salary increases, according to Bainbridge. However, in many cases the negotiating administrators' personal income levels are directly tied to the percentage increase awarded to the faculty. Even the most ethical and high-minded individuals must feel compromised when placed in such a position, says Bainbridge.[5]

"Students are suffering ... because of the district's financial management."[7]

Illinois State Superintendent of Education
Joseph A. Spanolo

At a conference on charter schools and technology in San Jose, California, several local education officials sat in the back of the room and quietly heckled each of the speakers. At one point, one of the individuals stepped up to the registration desk and announced that she was a school board member from the area, with ties to Campbell High School, and that she wanted her $75 registration fee back. "I thought this [conference] was supposed to be about what we do now. I don't know if I want to waste my time on things we should be doing," she said.

boards. In an effort to avoid such problems, Colorado's leaders set a good example with a message they sent to school board members. Persuasively, they suggested that members would be prudent to help with the charter movement rather than stand in its way.

Who's In Charge:

Administrators are represented by two national associations, the American Association of School Administrators and the American Federation of School Administrators. The National School Boards Association represents local boards' interests on a federal level and has approximately 95,000 individual school board members from over 15,000 districts.

What You Can Do:

As an individual, you can affect the school board in a variety of ways. You or your group can participate in elections. Through elections you can immediately influence how schools operate, in lieu of more widespread reform efforts. If you can find willing people to run, help them. If not, let candidates and current members know how you feel and what you are prepared to do in your efforts. Note, however, that most school boards have so little power that you should weigh seriously any consideration of personal involvement before jumping into a race. Another option is to serve as a resource bank for school board members. These folks often lack basic information and value your input.

To learn about school board members' views and the issues, make a point of knowing your school board's meeting schedule and attending regularly, or find someone who can. School boards are required by "Sunshine" laws to hold open meetings and to inform the public of meeting times and locations. They are also required to take public comment on policy issues. Unfortunately, school board meetings are often held during the business day when they conflict with most parents' schedules.

II. The School: Principals and Teachers

It may come as a surprise, but principals no longer run the show in our schools. Principals are forced to run their schools as higher-ups dictate everything from quality control of teachers to scheduling the school day to disciplining the students. The principal's autonomy and authority are determined by the superintendent and by whatever restrictions are imposed on him or her through government regulation.

Successful Principals

Principals can't pick the best teachers but must hire off restrictive lists. Even then, unlike principals in many successful systems, their hiring choices must be approved by the superintendent ... firings are almost impossible. Principals seeking to plan faculty meetings find they can't be scheduled because of heavy classroom commitments and tight union rules. Principals seeking to organize after-school activities have their plans vetoed by janitors, who won't keep the buildings open.

Amazingly, some Boston schools prosper nevertheless. Invariably this happens when an energetic and committed principal finds a way to bob and weave and ignore his or her way through the bureaucracy to assemble a group of dedicated teachers and to inspire them toward common goals.

Too often such principals find themselves pursued by central office functionaries. And when their schools excel, the success is often ignored.

Principals have gained some discretion and can invite specific teachers to apply for openings but still won't necessarily get them .... The process for dismissing incompetent or burned-out teachers is extremely difficult, as is the process for disciplining troublemakers among the students.

From the perspective of principals, the nettlesome constraints that entangle their efforts to deal with subordinates are no worse than the constraints from above.

One glaring example is the predicament of the Multicultural Middle College High School, a highly regarded adjunct of English High School operating at Roxbury Community College that is threatened with extinction because the administration says it didn't fill out the proper forms ... they must be doing something right because attendance is excellent and grades are improving. Theodore Sizer, a professor at Brown University, said, "Most of the schools that seem to work with kids break a lot of the bureaucratic rules because the bureaucratic rules are the problem."[8]

Likewise, teachers' hands are tied by so many rules and requirements from the local, state and federal levels that they're often reduced to providing little more than damage control from one 50 minute class to the next. Teachers are frustrated by such a system, and often bear the brunt of parents who are equally frustrated with their lack of control. Teachers unions have succeeded in ensuring job security for their members, but have removed the opportunity for teachers to be rewarded for doing well. Principals' hands are also tied by contracts that forbid them to reward good teachers or sanction poor ones. This sets up a natural antagonism between two groups already facing such incredible odds. Teachers are now measured not on how well they teach, but rather on their ability to process students through the system, ready or not, from one grade to the next until they either graduate or drop out. In addition, union-set pay scales are based on teachers' levels of education, their accumulation of professional development and continuing education courses and their seniority - all things that can have little effect on how well they actually do their job.

Often a first-year teacher's most valuable on-the-job training is learning how not to rock the boat and how to stick to the rules. A Southern California teacher reports that he was encouraged to spend less time before and after school with his students or he would anger the local union representatives and his principal. The extra time he was spending with the children was simply not in his contract. Another teacher in Los Angeles volunteered to type a new school newsletter. When the central administrative office learned about her extra efforts, they informed her that she was in violation of the district's employment contract - only "classified personnel" such as secretaries were permitted to type on behalf of the school.

Our system treats these teachers, who go beyond the call of duty, the same as it treats those who do not even meet basic requirements for the job. And the process that allows a principal to fire poor employees is too long and arduous for most to endure. Even when a teacher is successfully dismissed for poor performance, she or he is in most cases absorbed by the bureaucracy because the contract makes it too difficult to remove the person from the system altogether.

Who's In Charge:

The National Association of Secondary School Principals and the National Association of Elementary School Principals support principals through lobbying efforts and professional development services, such as publication distribution and workshops. Teacher associations oriented around professional development and curriculum, rather than collective bargaining and civil rights issues, include the National Council of Teachers in English and the National Science Teachers Association. The National Association of Professional Educators, Coalition for Independent Education Associations and the American Association of Educators in Private Practice offer alternatives to the two big unions. Teach for America and the Alliance for Catholic Education work to interest recent college graduates and those in other fields to devote two years to teaching in understaffed urban and rural areas.

What You Can Do:

Their frustration with their current situation is one reason you will find that teachers overwhelmingly support charter schools. Charters are normally free from collective bargaining requirements, and principals are free from constraints on hiring and firing. Many teachers relish the opportunity to enjoy a professional and productive work environment, and one in which they can be judged by the quality of their work.

One thing principals and teachers can do in the current system is to request waivers from their superiors from various burdensome requirements. Or they can create their own specialized programs in which children can choose to participate. Teachers who are free to innovate in an open system have accomplished much. New ideas are often not appre-

No longer can I remain silent! My long-held aversion to teacher tenure, which I believe has negative effects on the quality of public education, has finally festered.

I say, toss out the sacred cow of tenure. As a teacher of speech, drama and English, I have worked both full-time and part-time in grades K-12. I was in the educational trenches. As I walked the halls, it became obvious to me which teachers where effective and which were not; which ones were giving their best, continually growing as professionals, being innovative and stimulating learning; which ones were bored with their jobs, mediocre in their teaching, just collecting their pay, waiting to retire and sitting on their tenures. Tenure is antithetical to professionalism: there are few incentives for competition since the salary is set by years taught and not by excellence in teaching.

Let effective educators participate in a period performance review. Let rewards of salary increments go to those who go the extra mile ... periodic recertification of teachers should be required, and taking courses related to their field should be encouraged.

It is the teacher who is the key to education. It's the teacher with his or her gifts who can influence, inspire and spark learning in a student. Teaching talent is more important than tenure. Let us look to the heart of education by recognizing, rewarding and valuing the able teacher, not job security. Put the sacred cow of tenure out to pasture.[9]

ciated, however, and sometimes even mistrusted in today's school climate. That is why many outstanding teachers have chosen to leave their job security and have begun to contract their services to schools that want them. The American Association of Educators in Private Practice represents many of these teachers who are having success contracting to teach subjects from science to foreign language.

Meaningful education reform needs their support. Find out which teachers, principals and administrators are willing to listen and work with you, and ask them to assist you with information and public support.

I. State Superintendents, State Boards and State Departments of Education

The right and duty of providing education was given to the individual states by our founding fathers. In turn, states used to pass the lion's share of that responsibility to individual school districts. But now that more is being done and financed by the state, bringing with it, of course, additional entanglement, it is critical to know who's in charge.

State boards of education set broad educational policy for all districts in the state, on everything from standards and testing to teacher certification to the length of the school day and year. Often state legislation is needed to enact certain programs, but even alone, most state boards wield considerable power.

The state superintendent, or chief state school officer, generally manages the day-to-day oversight of a state's Department of Education. Sometimes called the commissioner of education, this individual maintains direct contact with the federal Department of Education and other federal offices and national groups.

The core of the state bureaucracy is the Department of Education, always a complicated maze of people and programs that have accumulated over time. Depending upon how state officials came to have their job, power and duties vary from state to state. Commissioners and state boards are often at odds. Particularly in states where commission-

About NASBE

The National Association of State Boards of Education is a national advocacy and service organization to which 42 of the 49 state boards belong. (Montana, North Dakota, Wyoming, New Hampshire, Idaho, Nevada and Florida boards do not belong to NASBE and Wisconsin does not have a state board of education.) Membership to NASBE is voluntary, and the organization is funded by board dues, which are allocated from each board's annual budget, as well as by public grants and contracts. With a 1994 budget of about $1 million, NASBE provides publications, training and orientation seminars, legislative conferences and issue study groups to its members.

The 1994 annual meeting for members included sessions on violence in the schools, bilingual education, curriculum standards and tracking, privatization, school finance and school-to-work programs. NASBE's stated goal is to strengthen boards of education within their state and increase their input into federal issues in Washington, D.C.

ers are elected and boards are appointed, they are forever quarreling over who is calling the shots, and who has what duties. The power distribution among the various bodies determines who wields the most influence in setting and enacting policy, and who merely serves as a rubber stamp for the governor and legislature.

How Your State Is Governed

Governance structure of state boards of education and state superintendents:

Across the nation, education governing bodies essentially conform to one of four basic models, as determined by the laws of the state. The following is a breakdown of the various power structures among these groups who together are responsible for governing teacher certification, high school graduation requirements, state testing and budget approval.

◆ In fourteen states, the governor appoints the board of education, and the board appoints the chief state school officer:

Alaska, Arkansas, Connecticut, Delaware, Illinois, Kentucky, Maryland, Massachusetts, Missouri, Rhode Island, Vermont, West Virginia, Mississippi, New Hampshire

◆ In a slight variation of this first model, in eleven states the governor appoints the board, and the chief state school officer is elected:

Arizona, California, Georgia, Idaho, Indiana, Montana, North Carolina, North Dakota, Oklahoma, Oregon, Wyoming

◆ In ten states, the governor appoints both the school board and chief state school officer:

Iowa, Maine, Minnesota, New Jersey, Pennsylvania, South Dakota, Tennessee, Virginia, Washington, Texas

◆ In the remaining fourteen states, the board of education is entirely or primarily an elected body, and in turn appoints the chief state school officer:

Alabama, Colorado, Florida, Hawaii, Kansas, Louisiana, Michigan, Nebraska, Nevada, New Mexico, New York, Ohio, South Carolina, Utah.

While some states deviate slightly from the above classifications, a general understanding of these basic models will help you determine the degree to which each official influences your state's policies, and the extent to which each should be accountable to the electorate.

Who's In Charge:

This upper echelon of the establishment is represented at the national level by the National Association of State Boards of Education (NASBE) and the Council of Chief State School Officers (CCSSO). In 1994, state boards paid anywhere from $9,000 to $22,000 to belong to NASBE. Superintendents paid from $14,000 to $32,000 to belong to CCSSO (in both cases money comes out of taxpayer funds distributed by the state legislature). Chiefs and state board members also are heavily represented on the boards of national policy and advocacy groups, from the National Education Goals Panel and the National Assessment of Educational Progress to the Chamber of Commerce's Center for Workforce Preparation.

What You Can Do:

In states that elect their boards, reformers have an opportunity to influence who gets elected, through campaign support and votes, and can always get involved by proposing, or becoming, candidates themselves. Boards that are appointed by their governor can sometimes be filled by committed individuals who want to play a prominent role in a state's reform efforts. Some states have strong superintendents whose election was to a large degree the handiwork of determined reformers.

You can also help your community understand the issues better by holding open meetings at which candidates or sitting commissioners and state board members can address the community. By providing such a forum, you make the candidates or officials aware that you are watching their efforts. (See "Chapter 14: Approaching Officials about Education Reform" for ideas on interviewing potential or present education officials on their positions.)

II. Parent Advocacy Groups: The National Congress of Parents and Teachers and the PTAs

Parent-teacher associations (PTA) or organizations (PTO) were created to involve parents in individual schools, and get them working closely with teachers. Founded in 1897, the National PTA includes over 27,000 local units with projects focusing on parental communication skills, drug prevention and both parental and student involvement. There was a time when the PTA was as wholesome as Mom and apple pie; the school bake sale funded much needed library books; and parents' input generally had a positive impact on the school's governance. How the times have changed! The national, state and large-district affiliates are now powerful allies of the teachers unions. The PTA has lost much of the "P" and is often dominated by people who already are part of the education establishment. Says the former head of the Pennsylvania PTA, "decisions are being made daily that affect [parents] but do not necessarily have their interests in mind."[1] The problem is that the PTA spends more time as a cheerleader, rather than a worker to change misguided policies.

PTAs influence and build public support for state and local education policy decisions; the National PTA is a strong backer of federal legislation that heaps more mandates on public schools. Like the unions, they have ready access to the grass roots, and enjoy the benefits of a national network of associations. PTAs can be powerful groups because they are perceived as non-partisan and apolitical. And yes, some parents are able to join very strong PTAs that are productive and helpful to the schools. Even when this is the case, the PTA should not be misconstrued as an organization interested in changing the status quo. Unfortunately, it should no longer be equated with Mom and apple pie.

Who's In Charge:

The National PTA is one of the largest volunteer education associations in the United States. It is comprised of nearly 7 million members and its headquarters is Chicago, Illinois. The association has two national conventions for members and one national legislative conference for its leaders every year. State affiliates hold a yearly convention, while local units use a variety of schedules. Home and School Associations that operate on a local or school basis are not part of such a state and national network.

What You Can Do:

Parents have no one national group to whom they can turn for guidance through this maze or partnership in reforming the schools. There are local civic groups, church groups, community associations and the like that may offer information, guidance and resources, but these groups, themselves, often turn to the PTA when they have concerns about education. Popular magazines or guidebooks refer parents to PTAs as a natural place to be involved.

Until the PTA is redefined to be responsive to parental interests, it will stay focused on protecting a failing system. Those frustrated by this are joining new or different groups such as taxpayer groups and non-establishment parent networks that are springing up in a number of states. Parents hold the key - not only to their child's success in school and in life - but to bring thoughtful change and grass roots guidance to their community and their state. Parents should never take their membership in any organization for granted, and one parent alone *does* have the power to make reform a reality. More about how later, in Section III: Working For Reform.

III. The Civil Liberties Organizations

Civil liberties and child advocacy groups are very active and influential in formulating school policy. While the public tends to think of these groups as champions of the underprivileged, they often defend the status quo. For example, the American Civil Liberties Union successfully defended a child's right to carry a weapon in Chicago, claiming it was a cultural icon. It also defended a student's right to wear clothing or hairstyles that school authorities judged disruptive and counterproductive to an atmosphere of learning. As a result, people continue to get hurt by a system the ACLU seeks to protect. These advocacy groups are often party to suits that oppose school choice, school finance reforms and any budget cuts.

Recently, these well-intentioned groups have been concerned with issues surrounding integration. Since the passage of Brown vs. Board of Education in 1954, many have focused on busing to ensure equality in education. The evidence often suggests, however, that forced integration has not lead to higher minority test scores, but actually to the resegregation of minorities.[2] Voluntary magnet schools and school-within-school programs that have relied on parental choice have yielded far greater success for disadvantaged children. The ACLU, with Americans United for the Separation of Church and State and the National Association for the Advancement of Colored People, are staunch opponents of school choice programs that help poor children attend private schools. There are still many people who believe these groups are helping and accurately representing the underprivileged. But, advocating for the right to wear clothing considered unacceptable by a particular community or using "free speech" rulings as a justifica-

At The NASBE Conference

At the 1994 annual convention of the National Association of State Boards of Education, the U.S. Department of Education Assistant Secretary for Civil Rights addressed the group on "Civil Rights in Education: Current and Emerging Trends." The Civil Rights Office, located in Washington, D.C., employs a staff of 830 and operates on a $58 million annual budget. According to the secretary's estimates, the office receives over 5,000 complaints a year and spends $28,000 per settlement to investigate and resolve possible civil rights violations in schools across the country.

The secretary listed several cases her office had worked on which she considered most noteworthy, including: a school where the girls' sports fields had no drinking fountains or lights, though the boys' fields did; a school with gender-segregated gym classes; a school that did not provide leadership roles for its pregnant students; a district that placed students with disabilities in private schools, resulting in their having a shorter class day; and, a school whose female students were not proportionately represented in after-school sports activities. These cases make clear that people who carry the "civil rights" banner do not necessarily have the most important interests in mind.

In another twist of logic, The Office of Civil Rights also filed a 1994 complaint against the State of Ohio for its ninth-grade proficiency test, which was being used as a condition of high school graduation. OCR determined that it needed to investigate "whether it's an educational necessity" to use such a test because a number of minority students had failed to pass the exam. After protest from state and national leaders, OCR dropped the complaint.

tion for offensive language and behavior, hardly helps those educators trying to make the schools work.

Testing is an issue that has drawn groups like the NAACP into the education reform discussion. For instance, the NAACP joined the Office of Civil Rights in its Ohio complaints. In 1994, Ohio introduced minimum standards tests for graduating high school seniors, set at a level of *ninth grade* proficiency. Of Cleveland's twelfth graders (only a third of the original ninth grade class), only 60% passed all four parts of the test - 76% of the white students; 60% of the African-American students. Despite the state superintendent's statement that test results correlated most strongly with school attendance, rather than race, the local NAACP president declared, "We are prepared to take whatever steps necessary, up to and including a lawsuit, to halt the administration both locally and statewide of this test to public school students on the basis that it violates their 14th Amendment Rights to Equal Protection of the Law."

The NAACP president vowed to use all methods necessary, "in the streets and in the court," including campaigning against any school tax increases, if the tests results were used to prevent minorities from graduating. Despite the fact that evidence shows people do better in school when there are high standards holding them accountable, the NAACP filed suit to get the test barred from use by the schools. The net effect of such actions too often is a lowering of standards and more court-ordered desegregation maneuvers, rather than working to improve the academic performance of minorities and paving the way for better schools in every neighborhood.

Who's In Charge:

The NAACP, ACLU, People for the American Way, Americans United for the Separation of Church and State, and the Urban League are among those who are often positioned against reform. Individual chapter members, however, may be more sympathetic.

What You Can Do:

There may be ground for agreement on some issues with advocacy groups, although traditionally they side with the establishment. But, just because they say they're for the underdog doesn't mean they are on your side. Make sure that members of your coalition know where these groups stand on the issues.

IV. Legislators and Governors

The action on education reform is clearly in the states - you will find the most significant efforts in state capitals. Many governors and state legislatures now understand the urgency for reform and have united to push effective measures. They have put the establishment on notice to shape up; their agendas include expanding opportunities for families and schools and eliminating burdensome and outmoded state laws.

State legislators rely heavily on national legislators' groups and each other for guidance. Many are members of one of two organizations, the National Council for State Legislatures and the American Legislative

Exchange Council, which exist to provide information and influence policy decisions. The NCSL signs up entire legislatures as members, while ALEC's members are individuals, who typically believe in limited government and local autonomy. NCSL provides regional and national forums for legislators, with a host of services including information seminars for various federal acts and topical speakers on select issues. These activities can have more direct influence on the outcome of legislation than most other factors. Both groups have positive dimensions, but NCSL is more comfortable with the education establishment, and their policy recommendations reflect that agenda.

Each year hundreds of new bills are introduced to create new programs, expand old ones and blindly infuse more money into education. Many that pass will have little beneficial effect on the schools. And, rarely do bills pass that get rid of programs which have outlived their usefulness. Most new laws have little effect on the quality of schools or the level of services provided, instead they impose more rules and mandates on how schools operate. Often, newly allocated money is eaten up by administrative bureaucracy and regulatory compliance before it ever gets to the classroom. Even the best of intentions do not get close to delivering better schools. There are some exceptions - those that focus strictly on cutting red tape. Charter laws, for example, provide relief from many regulatory burdens. Many states also allow waivers from rules upon request, but only a fraction of administrators care to endure what is a bureaucratic process in and of itself.

Educational flexibility is a key to good schools and needs to be addressed by the states. Schools need to be free to do their jobs. The problem is that the current bureaucracy was put in place by organizations whose very livelihood depends on keeping up that bureaucracy. Even if a state's governor with great support tries to cut back regulation, the blob continues to fight against such efforts to free the schools. For example, the California legislature actually released schools from bilingual education requirements recently, in an attempt to allow for some flexibility. The state's Department of Education, however, quickly wrote additional regulations destroying virtually all of the new flexibility for the program.

Some governors and education leaders want to change the way in which education is bought and paid for in the state, and they have championed reforms that address these issues head on. Yet, even well-intentioned lawmakers still become sidetracked by spending questions. The first issue is not to make sure more money gets spent, but to ensure that money is spent efficiently, on education rather than bureaucracy. The second is to hold schools accountable for our hard-earned tax dollars.

Who's In Charge:

In addition to ALEC and NCSL, the Colorado-based Education Commission of the States (ECS) and the National Governors Association (NGA) in Washington, D.C., also play a direct role in influencing the work of the states. Individual states dues to belong to NCSL in 1994 ranged from $62,000 to $325,000; the NGA dues ranged from $35,000 to $163,000; and ECS dues ranged from $35,000 to $105,000. As an individual member organization, ALEC charges $25 to state legislators.

What You Can Do:

State reform requires state legislation. Legislation requires support by legislators. People elect legislators. Sound simple? Despite this simple formula, citizens question their power to make a difference. In fact, state legislators are often persuaded on an issue by as few as twenty phone calls on the subject. There will always be those legislators who are immovable, but that is only because most lawmakers see the same groups day in and day out, lobbying for their own narrow interests.

Coalitions must spend time getting to know their local legislators and other elected officials. Many people take their state legislators for granted. Yet they are central in shaping education policy, and they want your input. If you spend the time to help them understand your concerns and get the full picture on the issues, you'll be putting them on the road toward legislation that will one day help fulfill your goals. Be informed and help them stay informed. Make sure they are getting a steady stream of information, news clippings and correspondence from you and other credible organizations. Section III will tell you what you can do to be an effective part of the legislative process.

8: The Federal Level

The Secretary of Education, the U.S. Department of Education and Congress

In the past thirty years, the role of the federal government has grown and created more bureaucracy and interference in local schools. Although the federal government says it takes a "hands off" approach to education, it gets states to conform to its agenda by tying education funds to compliance with regulations that extend beyond federal authority. Large research centers have been funded to provide guidance and ideas to schools, but in reality, they become promoters for pet projects that have little effect on the classroom. Perhaps even more harmful, the use of federal money gives the impression that such programs are federally tested and approved.

The degree to which Congress influences national education policy is directly related to who holds the White House. The Carter administration consolidated all federal education programs into the Department of Education; the Reagan administration returned some authority to the states. In 1994, the Clinton administration and the Congress once again increased oversight by mandating that states cannot receive certain federal funds unless they demonstrate they've provided the maximum resources. These "Opportunity to Learn Standards" focus on spending and social welfare issues that undercut high standards for both schools and students.

About Goals 2000

Goals 2000 proponents, like the NEA, argue that this program helps improve the schools because it provides additional funding for certain types of programs. The Clinton Administration emphasized that this cornerstone of their education efforts was strictly *voluntary*.

But according to the NEA, "One of its aims is that the standards and assessments states develop under Goals 2000 will steer other federal programs, such as Chapter 1. States, for example, will likely have to use their new standards and assessments as the basis for determing the success of Chapter 1 programs. Even states that don't participate in Goal 2000 will probably *have to develop* new standards and assessments in order to receive Chapter 1 money."

In the end, voluntary standards do become requirements.

Thoughts About the U.S. Department of Education:

The New York State School Boards Association believes it is time to reinvent the federal role in public education. The U.S. Department of Education should be eliminated and its responsibilities transferred to the appropriate human services department.

The Department of Education is far removed from the classroom and has become more of a burden to local school boards than a supportive partner. Using policy letters and program audits, the department has abused its authority by threatening to withhold federal dollars from states and school boards unless they comply with edicts devoid of regulatory, legislative, or judicial authority. The department has become a tool for interest groups to place mandates on school boards outside the legislative process that are unrelated to the needs of children. We urge the dismantling of the U.S. Education Department and the return of educational governance to local school boards.

New York State School Boards Association
Executive Director
Louis Grumet
School Board News, January 17, 1995

Since national goals were first developed in 1989, many new bureaucracies have been created to promote the goals and to ensure that states are attempting to meet certain standards. Even though laws emphasize the "voluntary" nature of the goals, funds are linked to a federal seal of approval. The intent to further federalize education is clear - as the Secretary of Education stated in a speech to the National School Board Association, "Education is back from the dead in Washington. Our budget is up $1.7 billion."

The issue of federal involvement is complicated, however. The federal role has increased, but it is not responsible for the whole host of problems in the nation's schools. The problem with education today is a mix of several factors. If the federal Department of Education were dismantled, the existing mandates would not necessarily change. One would first need to change the way federal money is distributed before it would have any impact on schools. When the department tries to influence local affairs, it can hamper the course of reform, and when it is antagonistic, it can stamp out sparks of progress. But normally, a strong state movement can survive any federal attacks, and good state legislation aimed at decentralization will fend off most federal interference.

Who's In Charge:

The secretary of education, a member of the President's cabinet, oversees the U.S. Department of Education. Specific committees in the Senate and the House handle the details of education legislation, and information and lobbying can be directed both here and toward your own senator or representative.

What You Can Do:

While your main focus should be on the states, you do need to keep aware of what federal mischief is going on. Put your group on the offensive by getting U.S. Department of Education press releases and statistical reports, and be sure to keep abreast, through your congressional representative and national groups, of upcoming legislation.

9: The Irony of Education Reform

Politics and Education

You can see from the great variety of groups involved, and the various power structures at work, the politics of education defies a simple sketch of who controls whom. Reform is more than a matter of bringing success stories to the local school board meeting or signing up with a well-meaning advocacy group. Sometimes those who wield power don't always win. And other times no amount of grass-roots canvassing can roll back a campaign of misinformation. But the sooner you get to know the players, understand their strategies and their agenda, learn where they'll compromise (and what can and cannot be compromised) and how to negotiate for - or demand - reforms that work, the closer you'll be to getting schools, and students, that succeed.

America's public education system is failing a majority of our children, yet many education groups scoff at the criticism that they are part of the "education establishment" - the blob - who fight not for change, but to maintain their positions in the current system.

True "education reformers," on the other hand, are those who work for reforms that improve the current system rather than preserve it. Education reformers are those who fight for the children and the future; the blob fights for the bureaucracy and the present. If you find yourself most comfortable with the first category, you're ready to become a true education reformer. But beware.

Education reform is not a business for the faint of heart. Many in the education establishment will attempt to make you look cold-hearted and antagonistic. Therefore, you must be clear from the start about what you want to accomplish and where the battle lines will be drawn. You must understand the nature of the beast before you try to take it on.

Positive, broadly supported programs such as charter schools, alternative certification for teachers, and school choice are just a few of the efforts being championed by reformers to improve schools. Yet reformers are constantly under attack by the education establishment for their efforts to get just such programs into their states. Although reform groups come in every conceivable political and social leaning, they are often dismissed, incorrectly, as "the right" or "radical right." (See Appendix II for a listing of reform groups). The liberal-leaning Progressive Policy Institute is just as reform-minded as the conservative-leaning State Policy Network, yet the establishment finds it convenient to type-cast anyone in the reform camp as right wing.

> The Center for Preservation of Public Education (an NEA department) and People for the American Way put out a Far Right Directory identifying the reformers they feel the need to watch. For more information or a copy of this scare tactic in action, call (202) 833-4000.

The opposition's ability to make the stereotype stick is weakening, and there are indications that opponents of reform are on the defensive. In desperate backlash, reform groups are being attacked more vigorously and viciously, and groups like the NEA have created special units to step up political action and muffle and disparage reformers. They've lost elections where they have invested a lot of money, labor and group loyalty, and they're under more scrutiny then ever before from the public at large.

To give you some idea of what you, as a reformer, may be subjected to, the following are examples of literature and rhetoric being used to divert and malign concerned parents and others who are trying to make progress.

I. On Scare Tactics:

Much of the material put out by state and local union affiliates concentrates on slandering new school board candidates who intend to challenge the status quo. For example, the Michigan Education Association put out an alarmist piece, parts of which are included below:

"'Christian' right extremists have regrouped in the '90s and formulated a new strategy: they're organizing at the local level, and their primary targets are school boards."

"It's very difficult to determine the extent of its organization in Minnesota, because part of the movement's strategy is to work quietly, to put an organization into place at the local level through evangelical and fundamental churches, then to surprise the political establishment by electing its candidates to school boards."

"The nationally organized fundamentalists have one agenda. They want to impose their strict uncompromising version of morality on a pluralistic majority."

"In Rochester, two fundamentalists ran for two positions on the school board last spring; one was successful. Backed by a local group called the Rochester Supporters of Value-Based Education, the successful candidate painted himself as a supporter of parental involvement and fiscal responsibility."

"But as a school board member, he seems to be against everything. He's against sex education. He's against outcome-based education. He wants everything back-to-the basics."

"Although 'Christian' right-wingers appear to be loosely organized in Minnesota, they pose a serious threat to public education nationally."

"Today's new right wants to do more than purge classrooms and libraries of materials and programs they find offensive. They are focusing on dismantling public education itself, with calls for public aid to private education, vouchers, and biblically-based curriculum. We must remember that this isn't a religious movement. It's a political movement."[1]

Sadly, these characterizations, often fraught with outright lies, are damaging to any group. With this "success," education associations continue to plan seminars that specifically address what words and tactics to use in beating back reform groups.

II. On Strategies:

The NEA has put together an entire department called the Center for the Preservation of Public Education, devoted to helping state and local affiliates stop reforms that diminish the unions' (not necessarily the teachers') power.[2] Reformers too should "be prepared."

"Just Crazies," says the NEA

"If there is one secret to successfully preventing the radical right from interfering with public education in your community, then that secret lies in one word: preparedness."

"Assume the worst. Assume that, sooner or later, the radical right will surface in YOUR schools, working to make them over to suit themselves. If you do this, you will take the time to work closely with a wide variety of organizations and individuals in your community, so that educators enjoy a favorable image in the community."

"What to Do When the Radical Right Appears"

"Understand that the positions held on both sides of whatever issue arises usually reflect fervent convictions; people holding them will not negotiate away or even compromise their beliefs. You probably won't be able to change your opponents' minds - so concentrate your energies on those who are either undecided or who are most inclined to be sympathetic to your viewpoint."

"When there are even the smallest stirrings in your community that smack of radical right activity, take the group or activity seriously, and right away. Do not assume they are "just crazies" and that no one will pay attention to them. That sort of casual attitude is how a small spark of trouble has the opportunity to turn into a bonfire."[3]

III. On Inflammatory Comments:

Some folks go out of their way to discredit those who threaten to expose their work or hold them accountable. A workshop called "Responding Democratically to Religious Agendas: Right-Wing Pressure Groups and School Reform" was held in Denver in May, 1993, at which the editor of the Oklahoma Observer in Oklahoma City spoke. Following are excerpts:

"One of the great battles in the Oklahoma Legislature was Representative Joan Greenwood, a leader... a teacher in a 'Christian' school. You notice I put quotation marks around that because someday God will get them for using His Son's name that way."

"Don't condemn a lot of these people out of hand. A lot of them may not have a Ph.D. or a lot of them might not have even finished high school, but they're people who love their kids and they love their public schools and you'd be terrified, too, if you sat in the pew of First Baptist Church ... and listened to a pastor talking about these godless, humanist teachers and this awful curriculum that was designed to do nothing but literally take these kids and grasp them from the jaws of God and put them in the pit of hell."

"You ought to hear the calls I've taken in Oklahoma City. That's where the retarded meet and greet and eat. The politically retarded. You ought to hear them: 'Isn't it true that the public schools are just demonic?' I said, 'Which little devil is this calling in?'"

"Ye shall know the truth and the truth shall make you free. See - I can quote the Bible. Wow! Or was it Donald Trump who said that? I'm never sure."

IV. On How to Know the Enemy is Near:

Groups who feel threatened with exposure will misconstrue any activity as a political conspiracy against them. They'll quickly try to make parental involvement into a dirty word. Here the Michigan Education Association takes very innocent and important parental activity and twists it to instill fear in its members. They declare:

"Forewarned is to be forearmed. Being alert to signals that warn of a Far Right presence is the basis of a school district's or local education association's ability to prevent or minimize Far Right attacks. The warning signs listed below are based on actual experiences.

♦ Unexpected classroom visits by parents.

♦ Increased attendance by same/similar groups of parents at local school board meetings.

♦ Demands for copies of documents/records under Freedom of Information Act.

♦ Demands to see instructional materials under the auspices of the Protection of Pupils' Rights Act, known as the Hatch Amendment.

♦ Attacks on sex and/or drug education.

♦ Unreasonable demands from parents to be involved in curriculum decisions."

Among the "Far Right issues" the MEA says members should warily watch out for: schools of choice; charter schools; sex education; certification standards; problem solving skills; decision making.

❖❖❖❖❖

No wonder so many teachers are confused about school reform! This kind of literature makes its way into their hands often with little to suggest the opposite. As you will find in your own community, a growing majority of teachers support the reforms that are being described in this Handbook. They are not part of the blob - they are the rank and file who care about kids. And they, and parents, are what this whole movement is about.

Now that you know the score, you're ready to get started on bringing better schools to your community. In the next section you'll learn what it takes to become an effective education reformer.

Working For Reform

Now that you know more about what's happening around the country in school reform, it's time to make that knowledge work for you and your community. And, now that you know the general power structures shaping today's schools, you're ready to find out details about your individual schools, to help them in their efforts or to steer them in a better direction.

Information is power. As with any business or private venture, information is critical to the success of any reform effort. Too often people overlook the complexity of education, from who's in control to what's actually happening in the schools. It is imperative to have information well in hand as you begin to make decisions about how and where to approach reform.

Whether you're planning to crusade for change, or are simply taking on the important work of helping your child through school, you must be an informed parent about education in general and your local schools in particular. Even if you have no choices to make right now and your child's schooling is satisfactory, a working knowledge of your schools may come in handy should you suddenly face the decision whether to place your child in one particular program or pull her from another. You will also be better prepared to evaluate issues that are regularly brought to the community for consideration, such as tax changes, conversions to charter schools and elections of education officials.

As you become involved with your local schools, you will find that those already in the education loop have the advantages on their side - whether they're working for change or against it. These people have access to facts and figures to support their position, and they have the respect, deservedly so, of the community's leaders. Take advantage of their resources to learn more about how your schools operate - use their expertise and access to get the information you need. As you begin to get a larger, clearer picture of how things work, use your own detective work to fill in the gaps. You will probably find that some of those education insiders will soon turn to you for the inside scoop on the issues.

What you need to know about your schools

First, get a general idea how your school operates and how it is performing academically. Write a letter to your district's superintendent requesting information on your community's individual schools. Ask for their standing compared to each other, to nearby districts and on a state level. Find out how they compare to other states and to national averages. Ask what tests are being used to determine such standings - by the school, the district and the state. Find out if the results of such tests are "normed," or curved, to account for demographic information, before they are used for comparison.

Don't be surprised - or satisfied - if the answers come back that your school or community is ranked above average, particularly on test scores. If test results are even made available, then too often they are at best misleading, or at worst, completely unintelligible. As one expert explains, "The people who produce our information about educational performance are, by and large, the same people who are running the system whose performance is being assessed. It is simply not in their interest to give clear, objective outcomes information; and, at least as we are currently structured, nobody else is in a position to do so. The upshot is that the information people get about outcomes - with a handful of happy exceptions - is the information that providers want them to have. And that information tends either to contain false good news - the so called "Lake Wobegon effect" - or to be so dense and confusing as to be unintelligible to ordinary mortals. Nor is it readily available for the level of analysis one needs. For example, we can now get pretty good national data about educational outcomes; however, almost no decisions about education are made nationally. At the levels where the rubber hits the road in terms of policy (state, local, specific schools, specific classrooms, specific children) it's very hard to get the necessary information."[1]

The emphasis in evaluating the schools has been focused too long on how much money we're spending, rather than how our students are doing. So the effort to find out just how they're doing has been haphazard and met with much opposition. "Most of the data we need, [to accurately judge our schools] we cannot get. Much of what we get, we cannot trust. Of that which we can trust, far too much is obsolete, unintelligible to laymen, or unsuited to crucial analyses and comparisons."[2]

So, it's time to start your own researching. Find out what you can about your school and where it fits into the larger picture. This is not simple. In addition to test scores, you will want information on your district on everything from money to demographics, to give you the complete schooling picture. The information you'll need will fall into the following seven categories:

1) Achievement: As discussed above, this can be one of the most

difficult measurements to get hold of and interpret. Assessments are generally done at the state and county levels, and students are normally tested anonymously, so that results aren't linked back to the individual, class or school. Most states require some form of state testing, and most districts and schools employ their own assessment tools. You'll want to know what measure your school uses to judge whether its own academic program is effective.

Also, children usually take a basic achievement test, the results of which are supposed to be confidential, and you should be able to get such information on your own child. Norm-referenced tests are employed to determine how well a group of students is doing compared to other groups. Throughout the country, tests such as the Stanford Achievement Test, The Iowa Test of Basic Skills, and The Comprehensive Test of Basic Skills are all used to assess progress in school, while the Scholastic Assessment Test (SAT) and the American College Testing (ACT) are used to assess progress at the end. But test scores alone don't tell the whole picture, partly because they tell us very little about what our children actually know and partly because there are other important factors. In addition to test scores, find out about:

◆ Dropout rates

◆ Graduation rates

Testing

Many parents have been concerned about certain states' new testing requirements. Each state is currently in the process of designing or already has adopted a statewide assessment that is mandatory for schools. While battles are being waged in communities over the content of some of these tests, parents do have a right in most areas to opt their children out of the tests. Whole communities in California opted out of that state's California Learning Assessment System (CLAS) because much of the test attempted to evaluate children based on very vague and subjective measurements. The outcry against CLAS was so wide-ranged that a broad cross section of lawmakers put a halt to its use until further review. It *is* possible to have an impact on programs in your state through a concerted effort. But you must know your facts and be prepared to answer tough questions with straight, objective answers.

◆ College enrollment rates

◆ Number of advance placement courses offered

◆ Number of remedial courses offered

◆ Status of bilingual education

◆ Curriculum graduation requirements

A century-old custodial system in New York has openly invited abuse. Custodians are allowed to administer their own budgets, are paid upwards of $80,000 a year, and often work second day jobs while hiring relatives to clean and maintain the schools. Custodians often have to mop cafeteria floors only once a week and have rules prohibiting them from painting higher than ten feet.[3]

2) Resource Allocation: When the education establishment talks about inputs, they're talking about money. But inputs, that is, things that cost money, are no guarantee of outputs, that is, how well students do. That's why when people say that the schools need more money to do a better job, you need to be prepared with the facts and figures on just how much money is already being spent, and how much of it is actually getting into the classrooms to benefit children.

Spending figures are generally broken down as follows:

◆ Spending on programs

◆ Per pupil spending by the school, the district and the state

◆ Average teacher salary

◆ Average class size (pupil/teacher ratio) - although this isn't a monetary figure, it is a direct result of 'inputs'

◆ District overhead - total budget and broken down for transportation, food services, maintenance and other services (compare this to the cost, quality, and method of delivery in other schools and districts)

◆ Central administration numbers and salaries

◆ Administration/teacher ratio

◆ Number of schools and school size

About Your School Budget

Getting information on school spending can be tedious and time consuming, but you need to make sure your tax dollars really are at work. In their book *Your Public Schools: What You Can Do to Help Them,* authors Barbara J. Hansen and Philip English Mackey lay out the nitty-gritty of what to look for and where to find it, as follows:

School funds are typically expended in six general categories: general operations (the bulk of the budget); special programs; food services; capital improvement; debt service; and extracurricular student activity. Each category will be divided into various functions or services. Each function is given a number. While the exact system may differ from district to district, the budget will be divided something like this:

Code	Function or Service
1000	Instructional Programs
1100	General Instruction
1200	Special Education, etc.
2000	Support Services
2100	Pupil
2200	Instructional Staff
2300	General Administration
2400	Pupil Transportation, etc.

Each function will be broken down into subcategories with related codes, such as:

1100	General Instruction
1110	Pre-School Programs
1120	Primary Programs
1130	Middle/Junior High Programs

Each of these will have line items indicating expenditures such as teacher salaries, substitute teacher expenditures and instructional supplies.

Compare with figures from past years in terms of percentage of total budget, rather than actual dollars - that will give you a better indication of where your district's educational priorities lie. Look at: percentage of the total budget allocated or expended on a particular code or function during a given year and over time; determine percentage increase or decrease from previous years, as well as the percentage of actual spending over or under budgeted amounts; determine the percentage of the total revenue in a category from each major source of revenue, compared over time, and the total percentage increase and decrease in each source of revenue over time.[4]

You'll want to know how the above figures compare to the previous year, the previous five years, the previous ten years, etc. How do these figures compare when adjusted for inflation?

If you live in a large urban area, is there a record of mismanagement? You'll want to find out if your district is in state receivership - that is, has the state taken over the financial responsibilities due to poor management and poor performance by the district? You'll want to know what court orders are in effect (such as desegregation or equity orders) that mandate where the money comes from or how it is spent.

Remember, these figures don't mean much in a vacuum. If spending has increased over a certain period, you'll then want to see if achievement levels have gone up proportionately. If not, why not? (And if not, as is often the case, then you'll know that more money is not necessarily the answer.)

Where to get the facts: School budgets are a good source of information on spending. The school board generally sets the budget; the superintendent administers it. You should be able to get your district's budget and previous years' budgets at the school board office or possibly through a local public or school library. In addition, the budget is usually presented at a public hearing - where you have a chance to voice your opinions - and the district may also publish a pamphlet or place an ad in the local newspaper to publicize the information before a vote. Your tax dollars are paying for the schools, and you have a right to the facts on how those dollars are being spent.

A separate but related topic is the source of funding. You want to know where the money comes from, both in absolute dollars and as a percentage of the total budget, and how this may have changed over the past year or decade. It will come overwhelmingly from the first three of the following five sources:

◆ Local funding

◆ State funding

◆ Federal programs including Chapter 1, Bilingual, Goals 2000, magnet school assistance, etc.

◆ Business/private partnerships

◆ Fund raising

3) Leadership: Who is it and how does it operate?

◆ District School Board Members: Are they elected or appointed, and how long is their term? What groups or individuals have endorsed the various members? When do they meet, and do they provide the public with access to those meetings or meeting minutes and decisions? What information about schools and the district do they provide to the public, and how? What committees do they have, and how do they pick citizens to serve on them?

◆ State Boards of Education: The same questions regarding the local boards apply to the State Board. Also, how much power does the State Board have? How does it operate in relation to the governor and the state superintendent?

◆ District Superintendents / Assistant Superintendents: How are they chosen? What kinds of contract stipulations do they have, etc.?

◆ State Superintendent: What is his/her general philosophy? Is he elected or appointed?

◆ Other governing boards: What other advisory or decision-making boards direct or influence the operation of schools in your district, and how do they operate?

◆ State Education Department: Who heads up the department, and to whom is it ultimately accountable? What information does it regularly provide to the public?

Assemble a list with office names and phone numbers so you'll have them at your fingertips whenever you need information. For more information on how to find out where your leaders stand on the issues, see Chapter 14: "Approaching Officials About Education Reform."

4) Policies and Programs: Once you know the players, find out how they're calling the game. Find out who stands where on the following issues, and any other issues that are of interest or concern in your community. Find out what is being supported, what sorts of partnerships or new efforts are underway, and what is being or has been blocked in your community.

Curriculum

When voicing concerns over curriculum and other school policies, parents often have difficulty getting a satisfactory response from their school principal or local board. The Independence Institute[5] offers some suggestions on how to approach education authorities to be taken seriously and have a positive influence:

◆ Find out exactly what's happening in the classroom and document it. Get hold of textbooks, workbooks, handouts and other media used in the classroom

◆ Communicate concerns to the teacher on a one-to-one basis

◆ Become informed: consult your library on the theoretical and practical studies available to support your position. Demonstrate exactly what the problem is

◆ Seek representation on textbook selection committees, curriculum committees, teacher selection committees and teacher evaluation committees

◆ Offer viable, responsible alternatives

◆ Teacher certification requirements, and "exceptions to the rule"

◆ Nature and status of teacher contracts, tenure policies, and policies governing teacher assignment, evaluation and dismissal

◆ Curriculum programs being proposed or implemented

◆ Policies on textbook selection

◆ Suspension and expulsion rules and their provisions

◆ Mandated course requirements, student performance contracts, community service requirements, or school dress codes

◆ Contracts with independent organizations

◆ Provisions for or existence of alternative school programs, including magnet schools, charter schools and schools-within- schools

5) Unions: As stated, unions wield much power on the local level, so you'll want to find out as much as you can about how they work and what particular issues they're working on.

◆ Overall organizational structure

◆ Leader of each local

◆ Union compensation to its officers

◆ Uniserv directors: 1,500 NEA field representatives are the liaison between the national organization and its 13,000 locals (They provide locals with collective bargaining and political assistance.)

◆ Information on the activities and contributions of the local, state and national union Political Action Committees (PACs), for elections and legislative issues in your district and state

◆ Union members serving on district and state board committees, or serving in elected or appointed public office (Find out just how closely the positions of these union members are tied to the positions of their union - they may or may not be beating the same drum.)

The NEA and its affiliates are be good sources of information on topics including average teacher salaries, enrollment and other figures, and annually published reports that include fairly reliable national and state figures.

6) Demographics: Issues of demographics are constantly being

used by those opposed to reforms. Apologists will blame poor school performance on the number of minorities or poor children in the district. Champions of the status quo will claim that changes to the system will upset racial balances or discriminate against the more disadvantaged. You need to know the facts to fight against these fictions.

◆ Number and demographics of students in special education programs

◆ Percentage of children on free or reduced-lunch program

◆ Ethnic breakdown of students

◆ Achievement measurements by ethnicity or family income level and achievement measurements by attendance rates

◆ SAT scores, with comparisons of achievement by racial minorities

◆ School safety figures, type and frequency of student discipline problems

7) Comparisons and Alternatives: What programs

currently exist in your district and state: charter schools, magnet schools, open enrollment or other transfer options, mandatory busing, etc.? How successful are these programs and what effect do they have on other schools and the district overall? Compare costs, achievement results, school safety, parent satisfaction, enrollment demographics, and other effects of competition.

Does the district contract with any non-government organizations to provide schooling (including mandatory remedial schooling or at-risk programs) or support services? How do costs and results compare to district-provided services? How do all these numbers compare to statistics for area private and parochial schools and alternative public schools that give parents choices?

If you are proposing a reform that involves private school alternatives, you will also want practical answers on how many private schools are in the area, tuition costs, accreditation, current and maximum possible enrollment, and information on resources and achievement levels.

The information you track down may be shaped by the information being put forth by the status quo. You will want to be able to respond to any misleading or false statements with facts and figures that will set things straight. Figure out what part of the story is not being told, and then get all the facts out in the open. Set straight any misleading or irrelevant statements designed to sway the public with emotion or half-truths. Acknowledge reasonable statements and support positive strategies being proposed by other organizations or by the school establishment.

Some groups will feel threatened by your objectives and will stop at nothing to make you look like the enemy. But if you can avoid these tug-of-wars, you can spend more time, and may have better success, implementing your solutions rather than debating the problems.

When you do get opposition, respond directly to their rhetoric and public relations. Use an attack as an opportunity to further publicize your mission. Demand equal time from the media and the public. (More on handling the media in Chapter 15.) Take the tough questions head-on and address people's doubts with the facts at hand - you are not selling perfection, just something better. Differentiate between what parents, teachers and the community really want for the education of their children versus the feel-good campaigns many spend time promoting. Don't get sidetracked into discussions about inclusion if the real issue is dropout rates. Don't be distracted by issues of multiculturalism if the real problem is poor minority achievement. Your public communication strategy is twofold: building awareness of the problems and providing a positive solution.

Your efforts will require investigation - so that you and your group know the facts cold, know the structures you'll be dealing with, and know what is already being done and what is being proposed. Be sure that you and others on your team are not stumbling over each other looking for the same information. There's enough material out there to warrant a division of labor.

There always will be naysayers and apologists who will give you a thousand excuses why things are this or that way, and why nothing can fix them. When it comes to problems in the schools, often those responsible will try to lay the blame elsewhere. They'll point to everything from the lack of funding, to parental apathy or student background to excuse the

"The Search"

typical search for information may look something like this trail through New York state's education offices:

For information on student achievement, you can approach your school principal, who may or may not release the school's results on standardized test scores. For comparisons with other schools in the district, a principal will refer you to the district's central office. There, someone will probably channel you to an assistant superintendent's office, which amasses district-wide information. In New York, each district produces a Comprehensive Assessment Report (CAR), which for the Albany district runs more than 80 pages. The report includes school-by-school statistics on enrollment, specific test score averages, graduation rates and attendance rates. Depending on the topic, however, some schools are merely identified by number, not allowing you to distinguish specific schools. No analysis accompanies the statistics either, and the presentation is not uniform, making it difficult to figure out just what all the numbers really indicate about school and student performance.

The CAR reports aside, ready comparisons from one school to the next are difficult, if not impossible, to obtain. The New York State Education Department puts together an annual report, "New York: The State of Learning" which provides comparisons between districts on issues from student demographics to teacher credentials. For any follow-up information on specific statistics, you would be referred to the Elementary and Secondary Education Department.

Financial information on individual schools is essentially unavailable at either the district or state level, and is only available at the discretion of individual schools. Poorly performing districts will voluntarily compile financial reports to justify how they spend their money, but New York does not make these reports available to the public.

schools' failure. Those who attempt to shrug off accountability for their job will have plenty of statistics and stereotyping to prove their point. You'll need to do your homework so that you know what the facts are.

How to Get the Facts

First go, as they say, straight to the horse's mouth. Approach your school principal, your district superintendent, and your state education agency for information on the schools. (See Appendix III for addresses) You may have to make several phone calls to any number of departments and wait weeks for your packet of information to arrive, but persistence and politeness should pay off. The set-up for each state, district or school varies, so be creative. Don't overlook the local or state union's public relations contact, who can also provide information. You might even try to get on their mailing list.

In addition, state and local citizens groups, research foundations and think tanks have a wealth of information at their fingertips.[6] They can help not only track down facts and figures, but interpret them. Many of these groups have researchers who work full-time on education and are highly knowledgeable on the politics and practices in your state. Your state or city Chamber of Commerce can be helpful with statistics and with practical information about the workings of your state. (They're also a good place to call if you need to find a hall to rent or want information about media outlets.) And last but not least, don't forget that your local library is an excellent source of information. Often librarians are willing and able to do extensive research for you for free, and can refer you to other places that hold public records.

You may be pleasantly surprised if your state is among the few that provides this information in an easily digestible format. The Texas Education Agency, for example, provides a small pocket-guide of "Texas Public School Statistics."[7] It contains everything from the amount of school revenues collected, overall enrollment (by grade and by ethnicity), dropout rates and even the percent of students who passed the Texas state assessment. If there's not something like this in your state, you may consider compiling one for your members and for the public at large. As you begin to build your coalition, it is this type of product that will make you stand out from the rest.

11: Building Coalitions for Reform: Laying the Groundwork

These are exciting times for school reform.

There are endless opportunities for change in the states and in your community. The key is seizing these opportunities and building the right coalition for change. Whether you already have a coalition, or are an individual who would like to work to change the climate of education in your community, there are simple things you can do to gain support and awareness for solid education reforms.

Who's Doing What In Your Community

Americans are united in their commitment to education. Find out which like-minded groups or individuals are active in your community, so that you can build on their work rather than try to reinvent the wheel. Nearly every community has a taxpayer association or other group interested in taxpayer rights. (See Appendix II on regional and national citizens' groups and education reform groups). Find out what local organizations, including veterans' groups, ethnic organizations, professional societies, civic associations and church groups, may be interested in building an alliance with you or may already be involved in a coalition. Approach these groups to find out what initiatives are being considered or supported in your community, and what new ideas might gain support.

In addition to groups devoted to a variety of issues, a number of specifically education-oriented groups exist in each community; some may even narrow their focus further, to look only at specific areas, such as curriculum, special education, testing or financial issues. Hope for Ohio's Children is one such group that deals with securing educational choice for parents. The CEO Foundation, headquartered in Arkansas, works with individuals to help them set up parental choice grant programs in their community. The Charter School Chronicle in Lansing, Michigan, tracks developments in charter schools. The American Textbook Council is a valuable resource to what's hot in curriculum issues.

What To Do Once You've Established Contact

You will need to decide whether you want to try to work through existing organizations you've identified, or whether your reform goals would be better served by establishing an independent organization under your control and direction. Obviously, depending on the scope of your mission, you will have more flexibility and control by establishing your own organization. However, such a commitment should not be taken lightly - education reform is not a short term project, and you will need to commit a great deal of time, energy and dedication to achieve success. Sloppy, rushed or half-hearted efforts could hurt your issues more than help them. The process is simple, but not easy. If you decide to take the plunge, a methodical and enthusiastic approach will yield results.

Building Your Organization

Once you've decided to take the plunge, assemble lists of names, addresses and phone numbers of local activists and potential donors who might be friendly to your cause. Your research on other community groups should have given you an introduction to some of the community's most respected and influential members, starting with the leaders of those groups. Scan every sector of your community for individuals who are active, resourceful and interested in the welfare of the community. For example, the Holiday Observers of Allendale, New Jersey, have for years put on public events for the town to celebrate each holiday; the Observers change from year to year and are usually pro-active business leaders who have the time and resources to devote to these events. Get plugged into these groups. Don't overlook groups just because their main focus seems social, professional, ethnic or religious. Such groups are filled with talented, involved people eager to have a stake in the well-being of

Janice Arnold Jones wanted answers about her district's spending habits, but found that the district wasn't very forthcoming. She learned that other parents in neighboring districts also felt they were being stonewalled by the schools on academic and budget issues. But the state's education reform law purported to encourage parent involvement and input. So she began to track down the newly forming parent groups and bring them together to meet, trade stories and ideas, and network. "News of the meeting spread by word of mouth," reported the St. Petersburg Times, and folks from at least nine counties showed up. "We're hoping this will be a way to give meaningful input into the areas that are most important ... these are just moms and dads and, in some cases, grandparents who feel that this is important," said Arnold Jones.[1]

How to Be Effective

As you begin to get involved in your community's school system, you want to be as effective as possible and get the most for your efforts. In their book, *Your Public Schools: What You Can Do to Help Them,* authors Barbara J. Hansen and Philip English Mackey offer advice on how to focus your efforts. We've listed some of them here:

- Distinguish between the public servants and the bureaucrats - those with a can-do attitude versus those with an armful of excuses about why they can't help you. Recruit the public servants to help you

- Don't accept excuses from those who have the power to change things. Be persistent and don't let them pass the buck

- Keep a sense of humor and don't lose your cool

- Learn when and where not to compromise

- Write things down and date your notes - summarize meetings and agreements, and distribute them to participants

- Never threaten something unless you are willing and able to carry it out

- Use multiple strategies to achieve your goals, and never lose sight of those goals

Your Public Schools highlights one very good example of how you, as an individual, can make a difference. Herb Green of Plainfield, New Jersey, became involved with the schools when his own children started going. He wanted to make sure the city's desegregation plan yielded not just more integrated, but better schools. He gained a reputation as an outspoken "rabble-rouser," was appointed to the school board and started a course to teach parents about the workings of the school system. Then, with a foundation grant, he formed Schoolwatch, a citizen's coalition linking education advocacy groups throughout the state. Schoolwatch testified to the legislature on issues, sent parent teams into communities to monitor superintendents' efforts and became a recognized, determined force in education policy. To continue Green's community education services, another independent group called The Institute for Citizen Involvement in Education was founded. The institute offered courses for neighboring cities covering topics such as school administration, discipline, testing, funding and teacher contracts, and was sponsored by local school boards or by grants in a number of locations. Some went on to organize improvement in their own districts. In the mid-80s, Green started up the Public Education Institute to continue and expand these educational services to the community.[2]

their community. You should always be updating this core "hit list" of individuals, no matter how established you've become.

• Pick your leadership team

From this "hit list" you will want to identify those few individuals who are as equally committed to your ideals as you and who are prepared to spend the time and energy to help you organize. These are the people you will want to recruit as organizational officers or board members. Consider how each individual can best contribute to the success of your mission, and don't hesitate to take advantage of the talent, influence or resources they put at your disposal. One may be a master organizer, another may have strong community connections or a dynamic public presence, another may be able to provide more money than time, or be a successful fund-raiser. Use the "capital" they have to offer, but "spend" wisely and well no one likes to feel his efforts have been wasted.

• Hold a preliminary organizational meeting

Organize an introductory meeting to chart your agenda, share information you've accumulated and seek advice and support for your efforts. Topics of discussion at this initial meeting include basics such as deciding upon a group name, recruiting additional board members, deciding upon a structure, division of labor and development of committees or task forces, the agenda, frequency of meetings and how often you'll stay in touch. You may want to draw up general bylaws to cover some of these issues. Define your philosophy and mission, and set a few basic short and long term goals. Determine the specific steps you need to take to achieve those goals. Devise your short-term tactics and your long-term strategies. Don't be afraid to revise your objectives down the road as the situation changes in your district - but don't be taken in by promises that will bring the schools only half-way to where you think they should be.

It's All In a Name

Pick a simple, easy-to-remember name that has very broad appeal. While you may have identified a fixed goal, it may take you many steps to get there. Connecting the name of your group too literally to one goal may limit your effectiveness or marginalize your appeal as you grow and diversify over time. A more generic name, on the other hand, allows you to recruit some fence sitters who may have been discouraged at the beginning if your focus seemed too narrow. Examples of good, broad names include titles like Parents for Better Education, Citizens for Equal Education, and Citizens United for Better Schools.

• Figure out the finances

Take up a collection for basic start-up costs, and ask everyone to contribute. People can donate funds or provide their donation through in-kind contributions, such as volunteering to copy meeting notices, donating the use of their phone, car or home, creating and copying stationery or fundraising. Set up a bank account to receive contributions and pay for literature. Designate two signers to the account - yourself and a treasurer.

Discuss potential supporters throughout the community. You do not need a lot of money to start; collecting $25 from ten people and getting in-kind contributions is enough to organize a small mailing and get the word out. Most groups initially attempt to fill their bank account by soliciting donations from a hand-picked group of individuals sympathetic to their cause. Later in this section you'll learn about reaching out to business leaders who are good prospects for donations.

You also can fund-raise through what is known as direct mail, in which you target specific people to whom you mail a letter or solicitation. There are people who do this for a living, but small groups usually choose to do it themselves. You'll need to find a friendly list to "prospect" for support. Possible sources for lists of names are community service organizations or other groups you've contacted so far. Such groups will have a directory that you may be able to get through a sympathetic member. Use these directories to pull together a small list, then mail a letter of introduction that includes a request for financial support.

Be sure your correspondence is brief, engaging and to the point. Always make sure your mailings look highly professional - use a computer or word processor with a high quality printer. Never use a typewriter, and never send out photo copies. Each piece of correspondence should be personally addressed, including the salutation, to the recipient. Include a self-addressed envelope to help increase the likelihood of a reply. If the recipients don't respond on the first or second go-round, don't despair. It can take a lot of contact before direct mail pays off.

Another tack is to plan a well-organized social or educational event. For example, you could hold your own education symposium and solicit donations from attendees. Choose a convenient but limited time, such as happy hour, serve light refreshments (always a good drawing card) and turn the gathering into a working session or how-to on school reform.

•Introduce your group to key community members

This first "open" organizational meeting will be broader than your initial meeting. You will want to expand your numbers two-fold and begin building your organization. Hold the meeting at a neutral location and make it clear from the outset that this is not your personal project - it is a community organization which is seeking additional members.

At this meeting, you will outline how the group came to be, its goals and any other issues that need to be discussed. This is a brainstorming session, primarily intended for networking. Send around a sign up sheet for names and numbers, which you will distribute later to all participants. Ask individuals to share names and numbers of others who perhaps could not attend but who may want to be involved.

Note: no coalition should seek to be a democracy. It should be made clear that although members' input is valued, the organization will be led by a core group of officers. Too many coalitions strive to provide equal say to all members, and thus set themselves up to fail or get sidetracked on marginal issues. Make it clear from the start who your leadership team is, and set up a formal mechanism for comment. Determine if there is general consensus among those at the initial meeting.

Expanding Your Base

Now that you've organized some of your allies and drawn up the basic guidelines of your organization, you'll want to begin systematically expanding your membership and developing your group's profile in the community. To do this, you will need to put together some informational and public relations material on your organization and the community. This is discussed in the next chapter in "First Impressions."

One of the first things you'll want to do is talk personally with community leaders to get their viewpoint and insights and to seek their endorsement. Some of those you will approach will be individuals from your ever-expanding "hit list" who weren't involved in the start-up of the organization. From them you will be seeking personal support and public endorsement for the organization, as well as leads on others who might want to get involved.

Endorsements

Endorsements are valuable because they give credibility to your group, indicate your broad appeal and establish you as an organization of consequence in the community. Endorsements can be used to help raise funds, indicated on letterhead, used when approaching officials, the media, and individuals from within or outside the community. Just one endorsement from a reputable local business executive or owner can bring a ten or twenty-fold return of supporters. Strong candidates for such endorsements come from among:

◆ Business leaders (bank presidents, real estate firms, technology firms, law firms, office supply companies, local grocery stores)

◆ Civic and church group leaders who are not readily identified with a particular cause or ideology (for example, in many cities, there are very strong and well-respected pastors of African-American churches who are sympathetic to school reform but not heavily involved with existing coalitions or easily stereotyped)

◆ Parents of public school students

◆ Public school teachers, principals and officials

◆ Concerned taxpayers

◆ Elected officials

As we discussed in Section II, most leaders of the various school associations probably will not take kindly to a reform effort of which they are not the primary architects. Nevertheless, there will be exceptions to this rule, and it is important that you try to win support from within the education community. If you get the cold shoulder from certain groups, at least you will know where they stand. But you may be surprised; the rank and file teachers and other education workers are very much in favor of expanding local control

A Warning on Collecting Endorsements

Be careful about endorsements from elected officials (or other prominent citizens). If you advertise an endorsement by a legislator known for a particular ideology, your group will be associated with that ideology, whether the association is accurate or not. Keep in mind that effective education reforms usually appeal to folks across party lines, and a partisan perception might turn off would-be supporters. Sometimes it may be more productive to take advantage of the personal assistance a legislator can give your group, rather than his or her name-recognition on your letterhead. Do ask your friendly legislator for advice on potential donors. He or she may have some ideas on where you can start prospecting.

and devising creative solutions to their woes. Often they know surprisingly little about specific issues relating to school reform; teachers and school board members are busy people and do not always have as much information as you may think, or the information they have may be one-sided. So while you may get flat out 'no's' from some, that brick wall may crumble once you get to know people, familiarize them with the facts and assure them that you are all working toward the same goal — educating kids.

Beyond your back door

Once you've identified key players in your area, make contact with national reform groups and involve their own local contacts in your efforts. The more national groups that know you exist, the more help and support you will find when you need it. They can provide you with extensive assistance in networking, resources and research information. While your focus is local and should remain so, you will want to tap into and be part of the network of reformers who are working on similar or related issues across the country. (See Appendix II: Organizational Resources)

12: Getting the Word Out

The First Impression

Now it is time to go into your community, inform them about your group, begin acting upon the suggestions and ideas that percolated at your first meeting and continue recruiting others to help you. Your introduction to the community has three objectives: You need to tell them about what your group does, why those efforts are needed in the community and what they can do to help.

Chapter 10, "Getting Informed," provides you with guidance about the kind of information you should have at your fingertips. The information you get will shape the message you bring to the community. Once you have that information, and have fashioned your message around it, you will systematically "roll out" your information campaign in the community. As mentioned above, your first target will be those groups and individuals you identified earlier who were not involved in the start-up of your organization.

Often a person's decision to support your position is influenced by whether or not your issue is already accepted by others. While charter schools, for example, may seem like a perfectly sound idea to you, some people may not have heard of it, or worse, may think it is a radical idea. To prove your position is a credible one, try to provide in the information you distribute any number of news clippings from reputable national and local publications. By showing that, for example, *The New York Times* believes in charter schools, you are helping that person come one step closer to your position.

For your one-on-one approaches you will want to present individuals with your plan for achieving your goals. Develop a basic business plan and sales pitch for presenting your group favorably. You should explain who is affiliated with you, what interests those people represent, your short and long term goals, and what has been done so far to realize them. Forecast where you'd like to be in about six months. Your goals should be modest. For example: DON'T say you'll have legislation passed during your first six months; DO say that you plan to reach out to all civic groups, school leaders, and other pertinent members of your community. (And then DO it.)

Writing Do's and Don'ts:

DO	Keep your writing bright and punchy
DON'T	Use jargon. You need to talk in terms that are easy to grasp.
DO	Use letterhead for all organization correspondence.
DON'T	Try to change the world (all at once). Focus your topic and be specific.
DO	Make sure your group's name, address and phone number are included on any group publications.
DON'T	Get bogged down in too many numbers or statistics.
DO	Explain clearly and concisely just what the numbers mean.
DO	Restate your mission and goals, and your purpose for writing.

Write up a short briefing paper or "white paper" on an issue or issues with which your group is concerned. Don't try to cover every angle of every issue - stick to the basics and keep focused. Include a few general statistics and a few well-chosen facts about the local situation, an illustrative anecdote or two, and a simple analysis and recommendation on the issue. All of this, no more than two or three pages in length. Keep in mind as you prepare the "white paper" that it will be the first document that people learning about your group. will read. Professionalism is critical.

If you are meeting individuals in person, bring this information with you. Never go empty handed, and always leave them with information and your phone number. And never leave "empty handed" either. Get a commitment from them to do something, even if it's just to meet or speak with you again at a later date. No one ever got anywhere by NOT asking for something.

If you are making contact by mail, send out your white paper with a one-page letter of introduction that provides a few key facts about the members, goals and activities of your group. Always invite your readers to respond to your letter in some way (i.e., call you for more information or attend an upcoming meeting). Indicate that you too will be getting back in touch with him or her to follow-up and answer any questions. And then, of course, DO it.

Keep in mind as you begin to approach people that many folks will be more receptive once you have officially launched your organization and have something concrete to show. Not to mention, going to them prematurely will make you appear amateurish, and they may not take you seriously. First impressions are critical - you may not get a second chance.

Sample Letter

Here is an example of an effective letter introducing an organization, with a simple and straightforward message:

Dear Ms. Jones:

The Friends for Better Education are devoted to providing excellent schools for our children. Because we all share this vision, it is important that we become familiar with the condition of our local schools.

Did you know that 54 percent of our children are not currently enrolled in a history course? Did you know that our teachers have little say over when and what kind of history they can teach?

Money that has been designated for our schools is not always making its way to the classroom. That is why we have formed the Friends for Better Education and hope you'll consider joining us in our efforts.

❖❖❖❖❖❖❖

Here is an example of bureaucratic language that you shouldn't use:

Dear Ms. Jones:

The Friends for Better Education was recently formed to articulate some direction and accountability to the dialogue of school reform. We are beginning to recognize the potential of a community to engage in positive contributions in our society.

We want to explore the affirmative role of schools in an ever increasingly technological society. In light of our mutual interest, the following data are important: Samples taken of school children indicate that 54 percent are currently not enrolled in a program of history. Professional educators are organizationally ignored, with little authority provided to them to determine curriculum.

Financial resources are misappropriated.

And so forth.

Following Through

After your initial meeting or letter, your follow-up contact should be direct - either a phone call or another meeting. From this second meeting, you should determine who can help you, and exactly what they can do. Even if they agree to no more than going on your mailing list and staying in touch, you've still scored a home run. You've made the connection. Now it's up to you to maintain it.

If you've found a true comrade-in-arms, explore to what degree she is willing to help. And ask if, in addition, she would be willing to give you several referrals of others you can approach. Perhaps she would agree to hold a small meeting or an informal luncheon to which she would invite a few select friends for you to meet and tell about your efforts.

Taking Action

Now you are ready to bring your message to the general public. The best way to do that is directly, face to face at a town meeting or other community forum, on the telephone or through a professional mailing.

Never underestimate the power of good public relations - or bad public relations. Today, everyone is pressed for time, and you may only have one or two shots to get folks interested in your issues and supportive of your agenda. You must always be putting your best foot forward.

DO: Nurture Effective Spokesmen and Women

While we all may want to be in the limelight, success depends upon taking advantage of each member's particular strengths. That means enlisting those people who really know how to sell the message to be your group's liaison to the public - and that may not include you. Spokespeople should be respected members of your community, have an ability to speak in plain language about your mission and your goals, and be able to answer the tough questions.

IF YOU DON'T HAVE SOMEONE LIKE THIS, YOU MUST FIND SOMEONE. A coalition that exists on good will but without sophisticated messengers will not survive very long.

DO: Host Public and Community Forums

Like the "everything is okay in public education" forums aimed at discouraging any deeper scrutiny of the system, your own forums should be held to give parents and community members a more accurate picture of their schools' state of affairs and strategies for improvement. Rent a local community hall or even the school auditorium. A town meeting or public discussion on "how our schools are doing" or "getting the scoop on changes in our schools" are two hooks to draw people. You do not want to be overly dramatic but at the same time you must be able to attract people who might have no idea that schools in their area have some problems or that any decent solutions exist.

To lend credibility and a broader perspective to the discussion, invite national and state speakers. A state policy group can often help you line up a speaker for an event either from its organization or network of contacts. (See Appendix II for a regional list of such groups.) Also, many national figures who travel may be able to provide you with a few hours of their time. Work around their schedules, and you'll have a dynamic, low-cost program that not only brings attention to education but to your specific efforts.

DO: Approach Civic Groups

Civic groups offer a ready-made forum through which you can publicize your message. Groups such as Rotary, Lions and Kiwanis clubs are deeply devoted to their communities and serve as excellent forums to get the word out about your efforts. When meeting civic leaders you will want to follow the basic rules outlined above and perhaps also try to identify a member who can say a few words and distribute literature on your behalf. Bring your group and your spokesperson to the attention of the organization's program chairman, who is always on the lookout for available and interesting speakers. Try to book your spokesperson for a luncheon speech, a banquet presentation or even a round-table meeting with the officers. Offer to help design a program around education, create a panel discussion, or even write a short piece for the group's newsletter. These appearances and meetings will help you gain visibility and support from folks who might not generally be plugged in to education issues.

Planning an Event

An excellent way to inform both the press and the public about the issues and your organization's activities is to hold public meetings. These can take the shape of an informative conference on a topic, a town meeting, a public debate, a panel discussion, a rally or a march. Following are some tips on what to do:

◆ Start early. Give yourself several months to plan the event and at least one or two months to publicize it.

◆ Get co-sponsors. Working with an established group will not only give your group credibility, but will lighten the load too - they probably already have experience holding public events.

◆ Get respected, recognized individuals to speak or moderate. Find out about any scheduled visits to your area by national leaders, and see if they'll take part in your event. Or invite a local editor or broadcast personality - this will further help your press contact. Line up your speakers well in advance, and confirm everything over the phone and in writing.

◆ Invite community leaders, education officials, state representatives and other respected citizens to attend as honored guests. Introduce or publicly greet them at the beginning of your forum. Perhaps invite them to say a few words - only if you know it will be in your favor.

◆ Pick a date, time and location. Hold your meeting at a convenient time for your prospective audience. Early evening is best for working parents and educators. Your Chamber of Commerce and local library can help you find public spaces for rent - choose a smaller rather than a larger room. An event in a small room with the audience lining the aisles and spilling out the back will look popular and well attended. Those same people scattered in the first few rows of a big lecture hall will give the impression that no one came.

◆ Get the word out. Give your event a catchy title or descriptive phrase that you can use to publicize it. Alert media daybooks and public calendars of the details. Distribute flyers, contact local schools and churches, talk to civic groups, mail to your list and see if other groups will mail to theirs for you. Get your group's members to commit to bringing ten people each. The night before the event, call around to remind your supporters and their friends to attend.

◆ Audio and/or video tape the event for transcribing later or at least for easy reference in the future. You may even want to put together a professional piece for distribution at a later date.

◆ Have an emcee. This person should be bright, cheery, professional and know the issues cold. He should keep the discussion moving and know how to step in if things get out of hand.

◆ Get the names, addresses and phone numbers of all those who attend and follow-up afterwards with a mailing.

DON'T: Rush to Make Political Statements

Politicking at the local level should be done only by those who have something concrete to offer candidates and those who have built broad coalitions. It can be a tough business unless your group is well organized, fairly large and well-heeled. Most people do not equate politics with education. Therefore, taking party sides (early on) can split your coalition and deter would-be supporters.

If you are thinking of stepping into the political arena, school board races might seem like the obvious place to begin. However, it should be noted that school board powers are so restricted by the bureaucracy above that you may not gain much for your efforts.

The wiser approach might be to establish contact with your local legislators and other elected officials. Legislators are often overwhelmed by the scope of issues they must rule on, with little reliable information and limited or no staff. By becoming a source of solid, objective information you go a long way toward gaining an advocate and achieving your goals. For more information on education officials and elected representatives, see Chapter 14, "Approaching Officials About Education Reform."

13: Growing Your Organization

After your organization is in place and rolling in the right direction, with support from a core group of community leaders, you'll want to broaden your base into the community at large. Staying in touch with people you've contacted and providing them with regular progress reports is essential. If you have laid the groundwork from the beginning, you will be in a strong position to gain broad support for your goals.

You'll want to begin a regular newsletter, and you'll need to determine who should receive it. This will be your primary means of communication with members, prospective members and your community. Remember that people love to pass on things they feel are worth reading. So while, for example, you mail to a list of only 100 people, many more may actually read your newsletter.

Your mailing list should include:

◆ Your supporters (moral as well as financial)

◆ Selected education leaders (school board, teachers, superintendent)

◆ LOTS of parents

◆ Officers of community groups, churches

◆ Business leaders

◆ Professional associations (local women executives, doctors, etc.)

◆ Friendly media

In the age of the information highway, there is always more information out there than people can track down, sift through or absorb. Establishing your group as a reliable, objective source of relevant information on education is perhaps the easiest, surest way of gaining credibility and influence within the community. If your newsletter gives information that folks understand, need and can use, you will be providing a critical service to those you most want to influence.

Teachers, for instance, do not generally receive, or even have access to good, relevant information about their profession. They are inundated with

Don't Underestimate the Power of Simple Grass Roots Activism:

◆ Set a goal to speak to at least one new person each day about your efforts. Also require your other board members to do so.

◆ Send letters of support and encouragement to legislators and leaders who take strong positions and positive actions for education reform.

◆ Don't give up on legislators and others who are not so supportive; make an effort to provide them with thoughtful information periodically, and follow-up with personal, amicable contact.

◆ Always strive to inform your community. Hold town meetings to make sure vital issues get discussed publicly and fairly; write thoughtful letters to the editor.

◆ Be positive! Always underscore your commitment to the schools and the children.

largely bureaucratic documents such as *Approaches to Teaching*, a book that "discusses the primary goal of teaching and helping students actualize their potential," or *Teachers' Voices for School Change*, which talks about political and social conditions in the classroom. These books, published by Teachers College Press, are representative of the body of knowledge typically marketed to teachers. Your organization can become particularly crucial to helping teachers get a handle on what is really meant by meaningful school reform.

What to Mail:

Your first newsletter should be no more than four pages long. Two sheets of paper printed front and back is ample space to tell what your organization is doing and still have room to include an article or two on the state of the schools, an important program or a simple reform philosophy. If you don't have a logo yet, get one now. It will help your group make its unique mark on the community.

Include short 'factoids' or 'quotable quotes' that are informative, funny or astonishing - and repeatable. Soon you will find readers who look forward to receiving, reading and sharing your mailings. In your newsletter invite readers to respond to issues or share information that they are uniquely able to provide. When you receive good material, mention it and the source in your next newsletter for the benefit of others. Always be sure to give credit where it is due.

Under no circumstances waste any resources to send out an amateurish or half-baked mailing. Wait until you have sufficient information, material resources and time to put together a first rate publication.

When to Mail:

Pick a time frame that is feasible for you. If you think you can keep up with a monthly deadline, do that and stick to it. If you are unsure, then start your newsletter as a quarterly or bimonthly mailing. You can always increase the frequency. To keep both you and your readers from burning out on the issues, don't mail more than once a month. If you need to circulate critical and time-sensitive information about a vote on legislation or a school board meeting for instance, send out a special alert before your next scheduled mailing — but do so sparingly, only when absolutely necessary.

Your communication with the press should follow standard protocol. See Chapter 15, "Creating a Program To Help The Media Work With You," to learn how to tackle press mailings.

Inform Yourself and Inform Others

They don't say information is power for nothing! The more information you can provide to the public, the press and elected officials, the more your message will get out. That is why it is critical to know details about your school system. (This topic is covered in detail in Chapter 10, "Getting Informed.") What is the per pupil spending? What is the average teacher salary? What is the school's (or district's) method of assessing how well students perform? What are the scores on these or other tests? How does your district compare to others? To the state? Nationwide?

Most important, find out about your opponents. How do the local unions and other education associations spend their dues? What have they said about accountability? Tenure? Renewing teacher contracts? School choice? Collective bargaining? What do they actually stand for? Use the facts you've gathered to rebut them head-on.

Do your homework. Know your facts, provide that information to your members and your community, and keep updated daily. Don't assume someone else is doing this. While there are numerous locations for good education information, you must dig it out, make it user-friendly and always have it in hand; don't just assume you can get it in a pinch when you need it.

It is possible to enact real education reform, despite the odds. Doing so requires determination, organization and a keen business sense. A wealth of groups and individuals are available to support your efforts. Remember: Reform is a mainstream issue, actively opposed only by people who have something at stake in maintaining the status quo. Effective organizations will get results.

14: Approaching Officials About Education Reform

All states and communities differ in their needs and approaches to reform. It is critical that those with official authority in the schools and the school system take a strong leadership role in introducing new and effective ideas to their communities. Superintendents, school board members and legislators need to be open and honest about their views on education reform, and parents, teachers and community members need to be vigilant about holding their education officials responsible for the schools. Part of your information search includes investigating where those in charge stand on reform and what they are willing to do to support their position.

There are a number of ways you can find out where these folks stand: public forums, campaign appearances, radio talk shows and other media. Use such opportunities to ask questions about the issues that concern you most, and air your views on how education officials can work in the best interests of the children and the schools. For school board, superintendent and state representative elections, take the time to learn the candidates' positions and recruit candidates with whom you agree to champion solid reforms if elected.

The National Education Association and other groups rigorously evaluate candidates from the local to the national level. You should do this too and share findings with others. Not only will you provide an invaluable service to coalition members, but you will also improve the public debate for the benefit of the entire community. And don't stop keeping track once the elections are over; once these folks are in office, they should be doubly accountable - they're now working for you, the taxpayer.

Find out where current education officials stand on the issues. Send them a questionnaire (include an addressed, stamped envelope in which they can return their responses), schedule an office or phone interview or take advantage of public forums and radio call-in programs to ask them the tough questions.

What to Ask of Your Officials?

Following are a handful of questions covering a range of education issues from achievement to spending to autonomy:

◆ What three education goals do you hope to accomplish during your tenure in office, and how will you accomplish them? Why are these goals the most important?

◆ Do you think reform can be achieved within current budgets, or do you think more money is needed? If so, where would you get it?

◆ What role do you see for parents in the education process? How much control do you think parents should have over the education of their children and the programs they're in?

◆ How do you feel about charter schools and other autonomous public schools? Do you see them as a viable option for improving achievement and accountability in our schools?

◆ What is your position on contracting school services to independent providers? How about contracting with private organizations to run an entire school, group of schools or district?

◆ How do you plan to improve the accountability of administrators, principals and teachers to our schools?

◆ How can we better assess achievement at the state, district, school, class and individual student levels?

◆ Do you support particular learning approaches such as back-to-basics, critical-thinking, outcome-based or cooperative learning? Why or why not?

Communicating With Your State Representatives

The most effective means of influencing the legislative process is by targeted communication from constituents to their legislators, especially to members of key committees deciding legislation.

The best hope for your issues is to find legislators who will champion your cause with their colleagues. One truly committed, determined legislator will advance your position much further than a whole group of half-hearted supporters, and will be likely to take advantage of your group's resources and keep you informed on developments.

Choose one suitable person to act as your group's legislative liaison. Although for logistical reasons this may not be your official spokesperson, the individual you choose should be knowledgeable and articulate on both the issues and the political process. This person can establish and maintain a personal relationship with legislators and staff that will make your group's influence more effective and consistent.[1]

Personal Meetings with Legislators

◆ Call in advance for an appointment, and explain your purpose and whom you represent. It is easier for the staff to arrange a meeting if they know what you wish to discuss and your relationship to the area or interests you represent.

◆ Be on time or a few minutes early. Since legislators have busy schedules, be prepared for delays and interruptions - they're inevitable.

◆ Plan on getting your message across in 5 to 10 minutes. Focus on the issue and be ready to answer questions clearly. Bring information and materials to the meeting to support your position.

◆ Be political: Legislators want to represent the best interests of their district or state. Show how your request will benefit the legislator's constituency. Offer the assistance of your group, and if appropriate ask for a commitment from the legislator on her position.

◆ Follow up meetings (and phone calls) with a thank you note and any requested information or updates.

Don't overlook the value of the legislator's staff. Often these folks focus on a particular area and are trusted advisors to their legislator on those issues. Keep them informed and contact them for updates on issues and bills.

A Note on Correspondence

You may want to organize a letter-writing campaign by your coalition to state legislators when education bills are being voted upon or are in committee or conference. It is a good idea to provide coalition members with a sample draft letter covering all the points you want to make, but members should personalize the letters they send. Each letter should be individually addressed to the appropriate legislator; postcards and form letters are less effective. And remember, do not send photocopies.

Format: State your purpose in the first paragraph. For specific legislation, refer to the bill by title and number. Limit your letter to one topic and one page. Clearly state what action you want your legislator to take.

Although written correspondence and face-to-face contact are most effective, when time restricted, constituents can call their legislator's office to voice their position or send a fax.

Approaching Fence-Sitters

You may not be able to change a legislator's mind, but respectful, informative and persuasive communication can go a long way toward softening his position. Legislation is always a result of political compromise; effectively articulating your viewpoint to lawmakers, whether they agree or not, is sure to work to your benefit.

15: Creating A Program To Help The Media Work With You

The care and feeding of the press is very important. Part of your job is to help them do their job. If you follow the advice below and stay in regular contact with the press, they'll come to view you as a valuable resource. They'll take your calls. They'll use your information. Someday, they may even quote you.

Newspaper reporters, broadcast journalists and the radio media are overwhelmed by the amount of material and information they receive on a regular basis. They are constantly being contacted by any number of groups trying to convince them that THEIR story is worth telling. So, as you begin courting the media, keep in mind that you are competing with everyone who has something to share with the public. The key to winning over the media is in establishing good relationships in which they can rely on you for information and assistance in reporting their education news.

Know How the Press Is Structured

Reporters come in all shapes and sizes, and so do media outlets. You must have a complete list of people who may be likely to cover education reform and your efforts. Making a list of media contacts is tedious and must be updated often, but it is critical to broad, effective press coverage. (In addition to the lists below, read newspaper and magazine mastheads and watch television program credits to give you other ideas about whom you should be contacting.) Titles to look for include:

Newspapers: Education reporter, city or metropolitan reporter, assignment editor, metro desk editor, editorial page editor, general editor and publisher. Don't overlook the free and weekly neighborhood papers.

Magazines: Feature editor, editor-in-chief and publisher.

TV: News desk, assignment editor, education reporter, special events producer and anchor. Start off with the local network affiliates rather than the national bureaus.

Radio: Executive producer, producer for a particular show and program host. Include both local and syndicated programs.

Wire Services: Contact the regional or state bureau, often located in the state capital. Include the Associated Press, United Press International, Reuters and Scripps Howard.

News organizations and larger television outlets:

Producers of news and feature shows at cable stations, both local and national, regularly sift through the information they get to find good stories. Include CNN and other regional or local cable programs on your list, and include them in any releases you might do.

A Note on Publications

When putting together your publications media contact list, go beyond the traditional local or regional newspapers. Publications like the *Indiana Business Magazine*, the *New York Journal* and the *Connecticut Magazine* serve a particular state or region. In addition, many areas have local focus newspapers, like the District of Columbia's *Washington Parent*, *The Citizen* and *City Paper*. These publications are often free to the public because they are supported by their advertisers. The advertising rates are cheaper than most large for-profit newspapers, and you might consider running an advertorial or an announcement about your group or an event. These types of publications are "community friendly," in that they target families, run listings of events in the area and highlight the work of local groups. Many times, these smaller papers are on a shoestring budget and look for contributions of stories. Often they cover local politics and education issues more in depth. Get in touch with their reporters and editorial board, and also consider contributing your own articles and essays.

First Contact With Local Media

After you have put together your media list, you will want to start making personal contacts. Begin with the editor or education reporter at your local or regional newspaper and with any feature writers who handle local "hot news" and human interest stories. If at all possible, set up a face-to-face meeting rather than a phone interview.

In this first meeting, you'll want to tell them about your group's agenda and goals, some key members of your team and their affiliations and some specific short-term projects. For example: "Our group's purpose is to help inform the public about their schools and how they can help to make them better. Board member Mrs. X is a teacher who supports giving educators professional authority in their classrooms. Supporter Mr. Y is head of the local Chamber of Commerce and is dedicated to raising our students' level of learning. We have collected X dollars to begin educating the people here in Smithville and plan to hold a town meeting on specific issues within the next few months. We hope to work closely with the school people, but we know this will be a sensitive issue as they may feel targeted. Let me tell you a bit more about why we formed and what we hope to achieve."

And that is where you begin the bulk of your sales pitch, based on hard facts, insightful anecdotes and testimony, and examples of successes either in your community or elsewhere. Remember, you want your organization viewed as a source for information, not propaganda.

You already may have met with or written to your local representative, whether a state legislator, a city council member or even the mayor. As we suggested earlier in discussing endorsements from elected officials, you may want to try to get a brief quote, policy suggestion or program support from your representative for public record. You can quote that official's policies or insights on education and reform to the media. Being able to "drop a name" to the media, with a quote on your organization's behalf, shows them you've done your homework and that you're connected to and supported by representatives of the people. You'll avoid the risk of being dismissed as just one more concerned parent on a personal crusade with no real power to change the system.

Follow Your Education Reporters

The key to developing a relationship with the media is in making frequent contact. It need not always be in person. You should develop a fax list and a mailing list, and frequently send communications updating media contacts on breaking local news, regional news and even national news that may not yet have reached them. (For tips on how to create and use news releases, see "Publicizing Your Organization or Event" later in this chapter.)

Writing A News Release

Following is an example of a local "hook" on a regional story:

Today, Pennsylvania enacted a new charter school law, bringing the number of states with this important school reform to 13. 10 more states are expected to vote on this issue within the next year.

Locally, the Committee for Better Education is working on bringing charter schools to the state and to the district. Says CBE president Joanna Johnson, "We're thrilled that Pennsylvania has joined the ranks of states providing local communities with the control they need to improve the schools. We'll be working closely with their leaders on doing the same here."

If, for example, you already have briefed a local newspaper reporter on charter schools and your efforts for them, then continue to keep them abreast of breaking stories in other states or regions. If you've learned that another state has just passed legislation, put out a brief news release headed with the words "MEDIA ALERT." Highlight the legislation's strong points and unique provisions, and then give the news a local spin, or "hook."

Make Your Pitch Unique and Informative

One critical fact you should keep in mind about the media: their coverage is shaped not only by what is newsworthy, but also by what will appeal to the broadest cross-section of people. They are on the lookout for unique stories with human interest and emotional appeal, and for startling but relevant information. They won't be interested in anything that seems self-serving or purely promotional, or something that simply serves to air your group's opinions on school reform.

If, for example, your issue is charter schools, focus on providing the media with the facts and examples about how and why charters work. Equally as important, point them in the direction of tangible, unusual examples of the charter concept in action - a teacher helping children learn in a new and exciting environment or a parent giving volunteer time to help make it happen. Put a human face on the facts and figures. If you don't have charters yet, but want the option for your community, illustrate the need with personal struggles: of the local teacher unable to do what he thinks is best in his classroom, of the children whose needs are no longer met by their assigned schools, or of the principal unable to release a disgruntled teacher.

Seek out the stories which are unique to your area but haven't yet received proper attention. Perhaps a local school board official has had a glimpse at some poorly managed aspect of the schools. Perhaps there is an example where money is not being spent responsibly - students stuck with outdated textbooks while the central office hires ten more staff members. The issues facing the schools are broad, and there are strong, concrete reasons why you have your particular agenda. Use the facts and examples to justify your reasons and support your agenda, not the other way around. The key to making your message known and winning people over - including the media - is in showing why you believe what you believe with real life examples, not with theory. You must draw a picture of what things are like, and what they could be like. If less than half of the kids in your local school are graduating with basic history knowledge, tell that story. If parents who ask to see the curriculum at a school are turned away by the principal, tell that, too.

Throughout the pages of this handbook, we've included real-life anecdotes and personal stories about good people doing good things and special interest groups trying to stand in their way. These have been included for your use and for your reference. Add to them your own local stories, and tell them to everyone you see. Most important, tell them to the media.

With the media, as with anyone you are trying to inform or influence, you must show that you know what's going on before you will be taken seriously. You must be sure that the stories you use are factual and can be verified. Do not share rumor with the press - it will put a quick end to any credibility or substantial future contact you could have with them. Remember, the reporter's name appears on her articles, her face and voice is on the television newscast. Each has a reputation to uphold and to build, and bad information compromises that.

A note on getting quoted: Always include in your news releases, perhaps lead with, a quote by your organization's leader, spokesperson or a recognized board member or supporter. Reporters are interested in giving all sides of a story, but they're also working against a deadline. Under such time constraints, they may not get a chance to call every source they want, and your news release or media alert may be the only contact they have with you. If you can provide them with a ready-made statement or mini-interview in the form of a news release, you'll be helping them get the whole story and, you'll increase your chances of being quoted or named as a source. With that in mind, make sure your quotes are informative, brief and catchy. Also, give credit to and quote from your information sources - it will reinforce that the issues are not far beyond your group and community.

Always continue broadening your network of incoming information, and you will soon become a valuable source of breaking news. For example, many organizations including The Center for Education Reform, the publisher of this handbook, send out media alerts and policy advisories to grass roots groups and other organizations to inform them about new and pressing developments in education reform. Go back to the list of national and regional organizations you assembled when you started to build your coalition and make sure you are on their mailing lists for policy papers and press releases; once aware of your education interests, they'll soon be sending a full supply of information from which you can pull.

Talking to the Press

There are a few important rules of thumb to follow if you're giving an interview or if you are called to comment on an issue or event. The first rule is always be prepared. In fact, every time you talk in public about your group's purpose and goals, think of it as an interview with the press. Being prepared is the most important part of doing your job.

That is why your constant goal should be to arm yourself with the facts and examples that support your positions. For each particular occasion, consider who your audience will be - local elected leaders, state school officials, parents, voters, educators - and prepare with their interests in mind. In a media interview, think about who will be reading that article or watching that program, and address their concerns. Focus your answers or your comments on what they would find interesting or noteworthy.

Prepare information in brief sentences or 'sound bites.' Out of a fifteen minute conversation, a reporter may use only a brief sentence or ten seconds of dialogue. Your chances of getting quoted are far greater if you give them brief statements that convey relevant information.

Be creative, but to the point. Use easy-to-grasp statistics, but don't confuse the point with too many numbers. Make your point, use an example or statistic to back it up, and move on to your next point. In a question and answer situation, answer the question fully, but don't ramble on. Know in advance what information you want to get across and don't get backed into a corner by narrow questions. If you feel uncomfortable or unprepared to answer a particularly pointed remark, use the question as an opportunity to make your own statement on a related issue. For example, if you are asked about funding for a multicultural curriculum, but are not certain about the details, respond by pointing out that the real issue is that x% of the district's budget never even makes it to the classroom level.

Become a referral source for information that may not be directly in your line of expertise. If you are able to direct reporters to other sources - both local and national - you'll be doing them a service that they will not forget, which will boost your credibility and increase your coverage down the line. In the case of our charter school example, when you're discussing the topic with a reporter, offer to put him or her in touch with a charter school principal in a neighboring state or with the legislator who wrote particularly good charter legislation that was just passed in another.

Always be mindful that reporters are usually working under a deadline. If they call you on Monday, the story may be scheduled for Tuesday's paper. If you missed their call, call back as soon as you get the message. If you promise to get them information, get it to them ASAP. If there has been a delay, call to let them know. And if you can't get it after all, by all means, call right away so they can keep looking. Never promise what you can't deliver - instead steer them to another source. If you leave them hanging, next time they will call elsewhere; in the process they may very well find a new, more reliable permanent source than you.

Don't say something that you would not want to see in print or hear repeated on the air. If there is something you want to say that you do not want quoted, tell them you are going "off the record" before you start, or tell them you'd be happy to talk to them "on background only." This kind of information can be just as good to reporters, if not better, than your live quote. And there is an unwritten code of ethics that the vast majority of reporters do respect when it comes to using such information.

When you provide your views on education reform, remember to tell the reporters that this is not an issue on which you stand alone. Although your group may be small or your name may be new to the reporter, let her know that many, many other people are working on similar issues around the country. Whether the issue is testing, school choice, teacher reforms or money, there are an abundance of people, statistics, and case studies to support the reforms discussed throughout the School Reform Handbook. Give your reporter the big picture - give examples of the specific leaders and organizations supporting these issues in other states and on the national level, including educators whenever possible, and stress the political and social diversity of these reformers. This will help you avoid being wrongly typecast as politically or socially narrow - or as just a lone voice on a doomed mission. (See Chapter 9, "The Irony of Education Reform," for further discussion.)

Editorial Board Meetings

In addition to meeting individually with reporters, you should set up informal discussions with editorial boards. Contact editorial page editors and tell them you want to come by at their convenience to inform them about your new group, your work or a local issue. If they can't give you a time and date for an initial meeting, tell them you'll call back when their schedule is freer. To entice them to take the meeting, you might consider bringing along a high profile supporter as a "drawing card" - but make sure you are in basic agreement about the issues to be discussed. Whatever it takes to get a meeting, remember, you must work with the press on THEIR terms, not yours.

Approach an editorial board meeting much as you would treat a one-on-one interview. Here, however, you will have the chance to flesh out the issues more broadly, to open up a dialogue and more fully present your point of view. If you find that those present are not sympathetic to your views, all is not lost; simply acknowledge that you might not see eye-to-eye on everything, and offer to keep in touch and provide regular information to them. You can still be of help to them, they will appreciate your candor, and you have left the door open for meetings at a later date.

On the surface, many in the local media may have the wrong impression of your group, precisely because of the depiction given by your opponents in the unions and elsewhere. Nothing counteracts such bad press as showing the media that you are part of the community, out there working for kids and schools. Write complimentary letters to chosen reporters when they report well. Call them personally when you disagree, or write a diplomatic note to the same effect. After such initial correspondence, call them to invite them for coffee with you or to address your group about education and their role in the media. Building alliances will have more far-reaching consequences than sitting back and criticizing the press.

Publicizing Your Organization or Event

One of the best ways to draw the media's attention to the issues is to hold public forums that they can attend or even participate in. Always let the media know about any meeting, informal or formal, that you would be willing to have them attend. It doesn't matter how large or small the event: the squeaky wheel gets the grease. The more you contact them, the better chance you stand of getting press coverage.

In addition, the media can be helpful in publicizing your event to the public at large. The following is a basic plan for getting both publicity and reporting:

◆ **Media or Daybook Advisory:** These one-page information sheets tell the media who, what, where and when. Send them out 2-6 weeks before the event and again one week before. Be sure to include a contact name and number. Some media outlets keep a daybook which the press and public can scan to see what events are going on. In addition to informing your regular press contact list, be sure to get into a media outlet's daybook.

◆ **Calendar of Events:** Know ahead which publications do calendars of community events and what day and time of the month those are published. Be sure to make their deadlines, and always provide a contact number for more information.

◆ **Story Pitch:** Find a hook and make a personal call to a friendly reporter to pitch a story that ties in with your event. Perhaps a parent or teacher is going to tell her particular story, or a national figure is speaking or coming to offer his support. Do not underestimate the power of a noteworthy or human-interest hook to bring in a friendly reporter. But be sure to pitch them the story you want to see. Do not leave it up to chance that they understand why you are calling.

◆ **News Release:** This is a timely, more detailed communication with the media. To follow up your media advisories, send out a news release for any event you hold, to be delivered or faxed the evening before the event, as well as distributed at the event. As with all communications, be clear and to the point. Include new or noteworthy information, the local implications of the story, and quotes from you or members of the community on the subject.

A Note on Press Conferences

You can use press conferences to announce: the official formation of your organization; the results of research conducted or sponsored by your organization; policy or legislative changes supported by your group; or any other significant development your organization has been involved with. Hold the press conference at a symbolic or significant location, preferably in the morning so that the media can run your story on the evening news or in the next day's paper. In addition to getting out the media advisory and the news release, call all your press contacts by 9 a.m. on the day of the conference to confirm that they're coming.

Be judicious in calling press conferences. Remember that news releases can be used very effectively on their own to inform the media, via fax or mail, about a breaking story. Don't hold a press conference if a news release and a few personal phone calls will get you equal or better results.

A Note on Talk Radio

Every broadcast area airs both national and local radio talk shows. They have a lot of airtime to fill and many local and regional shows continually search for interesting guests or unusual stories. Some may be very sympathetic to your efforts, while others may not. Pitch talk show hosts of both leanings, and get to know their producers - use the kinds of media efforts discussed above. In setting up radio broadcasts, it is important to objectively consider who in your organization is best qualified to speak in this forum; give consideration to speaking voice and conversational manner. Be honest: if it is not you, then act as the booking agent and let someone else do the interview. While you do not have to sound exciting to do a solid print interview, or even to give an effective TV sound bite, in the extended-time format of radio, you do have to sound better than the average speaker if you want to win over listeners. The main thing to remember is that you always want to be putting your organization's best foot forward.

Letters to the Editor and Op-Eds

Take full advantage of newspaper opportunities to voice your opinion or make your group known. You can use "Letters to the Editor" to clarify any press coverage about your group that may not have been clear or accurate, or to present more facts or alternative views to a newspaper report or editorial.

If you are responding to something already printed in the newspaper begin your "Letter to the Editor" with a reference to the article, including the article's headline and date. For example: "In your piece 'Shortchanging the Students,' January 2, 1995,...." You should present your main point in the first paragraph of the letter, then offer evidence to support your view in the body of the letter. The entire effort should be no more than two pages in length, and preferably only one.

Be sure to sign your name, and include all of your phone numbers, as the newspaper will want to verify that you wrote the letter. Use letterhead if you're writing on behalf of your group.

The opinion editorial, or op-ed, provides a larger forum for you to discuss your views about education reform or a more specific education issue. The chances of getting an op-ed placed in a newspaper increase greatly if it comes from a respected member of the community or someone involved directly with the schools. Try to enlist these people on your behalf. You can either have them write the piece themselves, if they are willing and able; you can ghostwrite it for their signature; or you can co-author it to appear under both your names.

The op-ed should be made up of brief paragraphs explaining the issue. To support your point of view use quotes of respected local leaders and recognized authorities, include relevant facts or statistics, and link the issue to local news or events. Below the signature line include a one sentence description of the author or authors and, if appropriate, their title and the group with which they are affiliated. Op-Eds should be no more than 600 to 700 words in length, always submitted with a title and double-spaced.

Use your coalition and media contacts to "shop," or sell, the op-ed to various print outlets, and ask some of your organizational friends to make contacts on your behalf. If you are not able to establish personal contact, you will need to send the piece with a cover letter briefly explaining the subject of the op-ed and its relevance to the paper or magazine's audience. Even if you are sending the piece "cold," to someone who doesn't know you, try to establish at least some contact in the editorial department so they'll know it's coming. Then be sure to follow-up with that person after you've sent it to make sure they've received it.

You may not always be successful, and you may have to try a dozen times or more, but with persistence you will get your views into the media and out to the public at large.

Conclusion

You **Can** Be a School Reformer

Maybe you've learned a lot from the School Reform Handbook. Maybe you're still not sure. Whatever your goal, whatever your inclination, you can be an effective reformer with a lot of information, a lot of energy and some good direction.

Remember, just because you think your own views are the ones that will work, not everyone knows the issues like you do, and many people are skeptical or suspicious of any new idea. With the media and with those you are trying to influence in your community, it is best to talk openly about all issues, rather than trying to sell them on just one in particular. Work to establish your organization as an overall education advocacy group within the community, rather than a group aligned to only one particular reform idea. Many of the ideas your group is pursuing will not be readily understood or liked by everyone — they may even seem quite controversial. Charter schools, for instance, are still a relatively new concept; testing and accountability are complex issues and most people think there are good mechanisms already in place; and while most people support the basic premise of school choice, there are many out there making it appear radical. If you are trying to wake-up and shake-up the system, chances are you'll have an uphill battle.

Win over the public and the media one step at a time. Attract them to you first, prove that you are credible, prove that you are working for the betterment of your community, and start painting a picture of what things would be like with your particular brand of school reform. But remember that even you still may be in the exploration stage of how things work, so don't sell the message that there is one easy way to solve the schools' problems. The public is wary of those who profess to have a silver bullet. Be broad, keep your goal in sight and pursue it carefully and determinedly.

Appendices

Appendix I:
National Education Statistics

NUMBER OF K-12 SCHOOLS: 109,228

NUMBER OF SCHOOL DISTRICTS: 15,025

NUMBER OF PUBLIC SCHOOLS: 84,538
Elementary: 59,015
Secondary: 20,406
Combined Schools: 2,325
Other: 2,792

NUMBER OF PRIVATE SCHOOLS: 24,690
Elementary: 15,701
Secondary: 2,467
Combined Schools: 6,522

Source: U.S. Dept. of Educ.: Digest of Education Statistics 1994, Table 5, Page 14 (1990-91); Table 89, Page 96 (1992-93).

K-12 ENROLLMENT: 49,819,000
Elementary: .36,170,000
Secondary: 13,649,000

PUBLIC SCHOOL ENROLLMENT: 44,254,000
Elementary: .31,837,000
Secondary: 12,417,000

PRIVATE SCHOOL ENROLLMENT: 5,565,000
Elementary: .4,333,000
Secondary: 1,232,000

Sources: U.S. Dept. of Educ.: Digest of Education Statistics 1994, Table 2, Page 11 (projected Fall 1994).

PUBLIC SCHOOL TEACHERS: 2,550,000
Elementary: 1,536,000
Secondary: 1,014,000

PRIVATE SCHOOL TEACHERS: 370,000
Elementary: 263,000
Secondary: 108,000

Sources: U.S. Dept. of Educ.: Digest of Education Statistics 1994, Table 4, Page 13 (projected 1994).

**PUBLIC SCHOOL
STUDENT-TEACHER RATIO: 18:1**
Elementary: 19:1
Secondary: 15:1

**PRIVATE SCHOOL
STUDENT-TEACHER RATIO: 15:1**
Elementary: 17:1
Secondary: 11:1

Source: U.S Dept. of Educ.: Digest of Education Statistics 1994, Table 64, Page 74 (projected 1994).

**AVERAGE PUBLIC SCHOOL PER PUPIL
EXPENDITURE: $5,734**

AVERAGE PRIVATE SCHOOL TUITION: $2,595
Elementary: $1,705
Secondary: $3,649
Combined: $3,853

Sources: U.S Dept. of Educ.: Digest of Education Statistics 1994, Table 165, Page 163 (1993-94); Table 61, Page 72 (1990-91).

**AVERAGE PUBLIC SCHOOL TEACHER BASE
SALARY: $31,296**

**AVERAGE PRIVATE SCHOOL TEACHER
BASE SALARY: $19,783**

Sources: U.S Dept. of Educ.: National Center for Education Statistics, "Schools and Staffing Survey, 1990-91."

**FUNDING OF PUBLIC EDUCATION BY
SOURCE:**
Federal: 6.6%
State: 46.4%
Local: 47.0%

Source: U.S Dept. of Educ.: Digest of Education Statistics 1994, Table 157, Page 152 (1991-92).

APPENDIX II: ORGANIZATIONAL RESOURCES

State Departments of Education

National

U.S. Department of Education
Office of Educational Research
and Improvement
555 New Jersey Ave., NW
Room 600
Washington, DC 20208-5530
(202) 219-2050

Alabama

State Department of Education
Gordon Persons Office Building
50 North Ripley Street
Montgomery, AL 36130-3901
(205) 242-9700

Alaska

State Department of Education
Goldbelt Building
PO Box F
Juneau, AK 99811
(907) 465-2800

Arizona

State Department of Education
1535 West Jefferson
Phoenix, AZ 85007
(602) 542-4361

Arkansas

State Department of Education
Four State Capitol Mall
Room 304A
Little Rock, AR 72201-1071
(501) 682-4204

California

State Department of Education
PO Box 944272
721 Capitol Mall
Sacramento, CA 95814
(916) 657-2451

Colorado

State Department of Education
201 East Colfax Ave.
Denver, CO 80203-1705
(303) 866-6600

Connecticut

State Department of Education
PO Box 2219
165 Capitol Ave.
State Office Building
Hartford, CT 06145
(203) 566-5061

Delaware

State Department of Public Information
PO Box 1402
Townsend Building
#279
Dover, DE 19903
(302) 739-4601

District of Columbia

District of Columbia Public Schools
The Presidential Building
415 12th Street, NW
Washington, DC 20004
(202) 724-4222

Florida

State Department of Education
Capitol Building
Room PL 116
Tallahassee, FL 32301
(904) 487-1785

Georgia

State Department of Education
2066 Twin Towers East
205 Butler Street
Atlanta, GA 30334
(404) 656-2800

Hawaii

State Department of Education
1390 Miller Street
#307
Honolulu, HI 96813
(808) 586-3310

Idaho

State Department of Education
Len B Jordan Office Building
650 West State Street
Boise, ID 83720
(208) 334-3300

Illinois

State Board of Education
100 North First Street
Springfield, IL 62777
(217) 782-2221

Indiana

State Department of Education
Room 229
State House
100 North Capitol Street
Indianapolis, IN 46024-2798
(317) 232-6610

Iowa

State Department of Education
Grimes State Office Building
East 14th and Grand Streets
Des Moines, IA 50319-0146
(515) 281-5294

Kansas

State Department of Education
120 East Tenth Street
Topeka, KS 66612
(913) 296-3201

Kentucky

State Department of Education
1725 Capitol Plaza Tower
Frankfort, KY 40601
(502) 564-4770

Louisiana

State Department of Education
PO Box 94064
626 North 4th Street
12th Floor
Baton Rouge, LA 70804-9064
(504) 342-3602

Maine

State Department of Education
State House Station No. 23
Augusta, ME 04333
(207) 289-5800

State Departments of Education

Maryland

State Department of Education
200 West Baltimore Street
Baltimore, MD 21201
(410) 333-2100

Massachusetts

State Department of Education
Quincy Center Plaza
1385 Hancock Street
Quincy, MA 02169
(617) 727-9173

Michigan

State Department of Education
PO Box 30008
608 West Allegan Street
Lansing, MI 48909
(517) 373-3354

Minnesota

State Department of Education
712 Capitol Square Building
550 Cedar Street
St. Paul, MN 55101
(612) 296-2358

Mississippi

State Department of Education
PO Box 771
550 High Street
Room 501
Jackson, MS 39205-0771
(601) 359-3513

Missouri

Department of Elementary and Secondary
Education
PO Box 480
205 Jefferson Street
6th Floor
Jefferson City, MO 65101
(314) 751-3469

Montana

Office of Public Instruction
106 State Capitol
Helena, MT 59620
(406) 444-6576

Nebraska

State Department of Education
301 Centennial Mall South
PO Box 94987
Lincoln, NE 68509
(402) 471-2465

Nevada

State Department of Education
Capitol Complex
400 West King Street
Carson City, NV 89710
(702) 687-3100

New Hampshire

State Department of Education
101 Pleasant Street
State Office Park South
Concord, NH 03301
(603) 271-3144

New Jersey

Department of Education
225 West State Street
CN 500
Trenton, NJ 08625-0500
(609) 292-4450

New Mexico

State Department of Education
Education Building
300 Don Gaspar
Santa Fe, NM 87501-2786
(505) 827-6635

New York

State Education Department
111 Education Building
Washington Avenue
Albany, NY 12234
(518) 474-5844

North Carolina

Department of Public Instruction
Education Building
116 West Edenton Street
Raleigh, NC 27603-1712
(919) 715-1000

North Dakota

State Department of Public Instruction
State Capitol Building
11th Floor
600 Boulevard Avenue East
Bismark, ND 58505-0440
(701) 224-2261

Ohio

State Department of Education
65 South Front Street
Room 808
Columbus, OH 43266-0308
(614) 466-3304

Oklahoma

Department of Education
Oliver Hodge Memorial Education Building
2500 North Lincoln Boulevard
Oklahoma City, OK 73105-4599
(405) 521-3301

Oregon

State Department of Education
700 Pringle Parkway, SE
Salem, OR 97310
(503) 378-3573

Pennsylvania

Department of Education
333 Market Street
10th Floor
Harrisburg, PA 17126-0333
(717) 787-5820

Rhode Island

Department of Education
22 Hayes Street
Providence, RI 02908
(401) 277-2031

South Carolina

State Department of Education
1006 Rutledge Building
1429 Senate Street
Columbia, SC 29201
(803) 734-8492

South Dakota

Division of Education
Department of Education and Cultural Affairs
700 Governors Drive
Pierre, SD 57501
(605) 773-3134

Tennessee

State Department of Education
100 Cordell Hull Building
Nashville, TN 37243-0375
(615) 741-2731

Texas

Texas Education Agency
William B Travis Building
1701 North Congress Avenue
Austin, TX 78701-1494
(512) 463-8985

Utah

State Office of Education
250 East 500 South
Salt Lake City, UT 84111
(801) 538-7510

Key Members of
The Education Establishment

Vermont

State Department of Education
120 State Street
Montpelier, VT 05602-2703
(802) 828-3135

Virginia

Department of Education
PO Box 6-Q
James Monroe Building
Fourteenth & Franklin Streets
Richmond, VA 23216-2060
(804) 225-2023

Washington

Superintendent of Public Instruction
Old Capitol Building
Washington & Legion
Olympia, WA 98504
(206) 586-6904

West Virginia

State Department of Education
1900 Washington Street
Building B
Room 358
Charleston, WV 25305
(304) 558-2681

Wisconsin

State Department of Public Instruction
General Executive Facility 3
125 South Webster Street
PO Box 7841
Madison, WI 53707
(608) 266-1771

Wyoming

State Department of Education
2300 Capitol Avenue
2nd Floor
Hathaway Building
Cheyenne, WY 82002
(307) 777-7675

**American Association of School
Administrators**
1801 N. Moore St.
Arlington, VA 22209
(703) 528-0700

**American Association of School Personnel
Administrators**
3336 Bradshaw Rd.
#250
Sacramento, CA 95827
(916) 362-0300

**American Federation of School
Administrators**
1729 21st St., N.W.
Washington, D.C. 20009-1101
(202) 986-4209

American Federation of Teachers
555 New Jersey Avenue, N.W.
Washington, D.C. 20001
(202) 879-4400
(800) 238-1133

Council of Chief State School Officers
1 Massachusetts Ave., N.W.
Suite 700
Washington, D.C. 20001-1431
(202) 408-5505

Council of Great City Schools
1301 Pennsylvania Avenue, NW
Sute 702
Washington, DC 20004
(202) 393-2427

Education Commission of the States
707 17th Street, Suite 2700
Denver, CO 80202
(303) 299-3600

**National Association of Elementary School
Principals**
1615 Duke St.
Alexandria, VA 22314-3483
(703) 684-3345

**National Association of Secondary School
Principals**
1904 Association Drive
Reston, VA 22091
(703) 860-0200

**National Association of State Boards of
Education**
1012 Cameron St.
Alexandria, VA 22314
(703) 684-4000

National Council of Teachers of English
1111 West Kenyon Road
Urbana, IL 61801
(217) 328-3870

National Education Association
1201 16th Street, N.W.
Washington, D.C. 20036
(202) 833-4000

National Education Goals Panel
1850 M St., N.W.
Suite 270
Washington, D.C. 20036
(202) 632-0952

The National Parent Teachers Association
700 N. Rush St.
Chicago, IL 60611-2571
(312) 670-6782

National School Boards Association
1680 Duke St.
Alexandria, VA 22314
(703) 838-6722

**National School Public Relations
Administrators**
1501 Lee Highway
Suite 201
Arlington, VA 22209
(703) 528-5840

Private Scholarship Programs

National

CEO AMERICA
P.O. Box 1543
Bentonville, AR 72712-1543
(501) 273-6957

The National Scholarship Center
One Massachusetts Ave., NW
Suite 330
Washington, DC 20001
(202) 842-1355

Arizona

Arizona School Choice Trust, Inc.
29201 N. 114 Street
Scottsdale, AZ 85262
(602) 585-0667

Arkansas

Free to Choose
P.O. Box 3686
Little Rock, AR 72203
(501) 931-7440

California

CEO of Southern California
P.O. Box 459
Cerritos, CA 90702-0459
(310) 407-1538

CEO Foundation /Oakland
P.O. Box 14068
Oakland, CA 94614
(510) 483-7971

Education Foundation
Archdiocese of Los Angeles
1531 West Ninth Street
Los Angeles, CA 90015-1194
(213) 251-2635

Colorado

Educational Options for Children
P.O. Box 4729
Denver, CO 80204
(303) 371-1370

District of Columbia

Washington Scholarship Fund
One Massachusetts Ave., NW
Suite 330
Washington, DC 20001
(202) 842-1355

District of Columbia/Maryland

Charity for Choice
P.O. Box 327
Temple Hills, MD 20757
(301) 899-6479

Georgia

Children's Education Foundation
3060 Peachtree Road, NW
19th Floor
Atlanta, GA 30305
(404) 814-5214

Indiana

CHOICE Charitable Trust
c/o Golden Rule Insurance Co.
7440 Woodland Drive
Indianapolis, Indiana 46278-1719
(317) 293-7600

Massachusetts

Catholic Schools Foundation, Inc.
Inner-City Scholarship Fund
2121 Commonwealth Ave.
Brighton, MA 02135-3193
(617) 254-0100

Michigan

Vandenberg Foundation
126 Ottawa, NW
Suite 600
Grand Rapids, MI 49503
(616) 459-2222

New Jersey

Scholarship Fund for Inner-City Children
31 Mulberry Street
Newark, New Jersey 07102
(201) 596-4313

New York

Student/Sponsor Partnership
420 Lexington Ave.
Suite 2930
New York, NY 10017
(212) 986-9575

Hope through Education
Social Renewal Foundation
P.O. Box 6
Philmont, NY 12565
(518) 672-5605

Operation Exodus
27 West 47th Street
Room 207
New York, NY 10036
(212) 391-8059

Texas

San Antonio CEO Foundation
8122 Datapoint Drive, Suite 300
San Antonio, Texas 78229
(210) 614-0037

Austin CEO Foundation
111 Congress Avenue, Suite 300
Austin, Texas 78701
(512) 472-0153

Children's Education Fund
P.O. Box 381029
Duncanville, TX 75138
(214) 298-4211

The Houston CEO Foundation
712 9th Street
Suite 2200
Houston, TX 77002
(713) 546-2515

CEO Foundation/ Midland
P.O. Box 50588
Midland, TX 79710
(915) 699-6065

Wisconsin

Partners Advancing Values in Education (PAVE)
1434 West State Street
Milwaukee, WI 53233
(414) 342-1505

Professional Groups

American Association of Educators In Private Practice
N7425 Switzke Road
Watertown, WI 53094
(800) 252-3280 or
(414) 475-2436

American Association of Christian Schools
P.O. Box 2189
Independence, MO 64055
(816) 795-7709

American Legislative Exchange Council
910 17th St., NW
5th floor
Washington, DC 20006
(202) 466-3800

American Textbook Council
475 Riverside Drive
#518
New York, NY 10115-0518
(212) 870-2760

Associated Professional Educators of Louisiana
P.O. Box 14265
Baton Rouge, LA 70898
(504) 769-4005 or
(800) 364-2735

Association for Effective Schools, Inc.
8250 Sharpton Road
R.D. Box 143
Stuyvesant, NY 12173
(518) 758-9828

Coalition for Independent Education Associations
1212 South Boulevard, Suite 101-A
Charlotte, NC 28230
(704) 335-0089

Core Knowledge Foundation
2012-B Morton Drive
Charlottesville, Va 22903
(804) 977-7550

Council for American Private Education
1726 M Street, NW
Suite 703
Washington, DC 20036-4502
(202) 659-0016

Council for Basic Education
1319 F Street, NW
Suite 900
Washington, DC 20004-1152
(202) 347-4171

Educational Excellence Network
Herman Kahn Center
P.O. Box 26-919
Indianapolis, IN 46226
(317) 545-1000

Institute for Educational Leadership
1001 Connecticut Ave., NW
Suite 310
Washington, DC 20036
(202) 822-8405

National Assessment Governing Board
(administers National Assessment of Educational Progress)
800 North Capitol Street, NW
Suite 825
Washington, DC 20002-4233
(202) 357-6938

National Association of Independent Schools
1620 L Street, NW
Washington, DC 20036-5605
(202) 973-9700

National Association of Professional Educators
13354 Copperstone
Sun City West, AZ 85375
(602) 584-4920

National Catholic Educational Association
1077 30th Street, NW
Suite 100
Washington, DC 20007
(202) 337-6232

National Center for Accelerated Schools Project
Stanford University
CERAS 109
Stanford, CA 94305-3084
(415) 725-1676

National Council for History Education, Inc.
26915 Westwood Road
Suite B-2
Westlake, OH 44145-4656
(216) 835-1776

National Council of State Legislatures
1560 Broadway, Ste. 700
Denver, CO 80202
(303) 830-2200

National Independent Private Schools Association
6210 17th Avenue West
Bradenton, FL 34209
(813) 798-3621

National Science Teacher Association
1840 Wilson Boulevard
Arlington, VA 22201
(703) 243-7100

Progressive Policy Institute
518 C Street, NE
Washington, DC 20002
(202) 547-0001

State Policy Network
816 Mill Lake Road
Fort Wayne, IN 46845-6400
(219) 637-7778

Teach For America
20 Exchange Place 8th Floor
New York, NY 10005
(212) 425-9039

The Alliance for Catholic Education
University of Notre Dame
0322 Hesburgh Center
Notre Dame, IN 46556
(219) 631-7052

Education Reform Groups

NORTHEAST

Coalition for Educational Choice
43K Stoney Run
Maple Shade, NJ 08052
(609) 231-0775

Coalition of Essential Schools
Brown University
Box 1969
Providence, RI 02912
(401) 863-3384

Committee to Save Our Schools
P.O. Box 5222
Westport, CT 06881
(203) 454-7283

The Empire Foundation
130 Washington Avenue
Suite 1000
Albany, NY 12210
(518) 432-4444

Ethan Allen Institute
PO Box 117
South Ryegate, VT 05069-0117
(802) 695-2555

Maine School Choice Coalition
12 Belmont Street
Brunswick, ME 04011
(207) 729-1590

Manhattan Instritute
Center for Education Innovation
52 Vanderbilt Avenue
New York, NY 10017
(212) 599-7000

New York Citizens for a Sound Economy
P.O. Box 596
Manorville, NY 11949
(516) 874-8353

Pennsylvania Leadership Council
223 State Street
Harrisburg, PA 17101
(717) 232-5919

Pioneer Institute for Public Policy Research
Charter School Resource Center
85 Devonshire Street
8th Floor
Boston, MA 02109
(617) 723-2277

Public Affairs Research Institute of New Jersey
212 Carnegie Center
Suite 100
Princeton, NJ 08540-6236
(609) 452-0220

REACH Alliance
P.O. Box 1283
600 North Second Street, #400
Harrisburg, PA 17108-1283
(717) 238-1878

Yankee Institute
117 London Turnpike
Glastonbury, CT 06033
(203) 633-8188

MID-ATLANTIC

Delaware Public Policy Institute
One Commerce Center, #200
12th and Orange Streets
Wilimington, DE 19801-5401
(302) 655-7221

The Empowerment Network
2210 Mt. Vernon Ave.
Suite 301
Alexandria, VA 22301
(703) 548-6812

Institute for Justice
1001 Pennsylvania Avenue, NW
Suite 200-South
Washington, DC 20004-2505
(202) 457-4240

West Virginia Family Council
906 20th Street
Huntington, WV 25703
(304) 736-1187

SOUTHEAST

Alabama Family Alliance
402 Office Park Drive
Suite 300
Birmingham, AL 35223-2416
(205) 870-9900

Alternative Public Schools, Inc.
28 White Bridge Road
Nashville, TN 37205
(615) 352-2080

Floridians for Educational Choice
P.O. Box 13894
Tallahassee, FL 32317
(904) 422-2179

Georgia Parents for Better Education
1355 Peachtree Street, NE
Suite 1150
Atlanta, GA 30309
(404) 876-3335

Georgia Public Policy Foundation
2900 Chamblee-Tucker Road
Building #6
Atlanta, GA 30341-4128
(404) 455-7600

The James Madison Institute for Public Policy Studies
P.O. Box 13894
Tallahassee, FL 32317-3894
(904) 386-3131

John Locke Foundation
P.O. Box 17822
6512 Six Forks Roads, Suite 203B
Raleigh, NC 27612
(919) 847-2690

Lousiana Association of Business and

Industry
3113 Valley Creek Drive
Baton Rouge, LA 70808
(504) 928-5388

South Carolina Policy Council
1419 Pendleton Street
Columbia, SC 29201-2047
(803) 779-5022

Tennesseans for Competitive Schools
P.O. Box 2647
Nashville, TN 37219
(800) 841-0006

MIDWEST

The Buckeye Center for Public Policy Solutions
131 N. Ludlow Street
Suite 308
Dayton, OH 45402
(513) 224-8352

The Blum Center for Parental Freedom in Education
Marquette University
Brooks Hall #209
Milwaukee, WI 53233
(414) 288-3170

Center of the American Experiment
2342 Plaza VII
45 South 7th Street
Minneapolis, MN 55402
(612) 338-3605

Center for Policy Studies
59 West Fourth Street
St. Paul, MN 55102
(612) 224-9703

Center for School Change
Humphrey Institute of Public Affairs
University of Minnesota
301 19th Avenue South
Minneapolis, MN 55455
(612) 625-3506

Charter School Center
210 West Grant Street, Suite 321
Minneapolis, MN 55403
(612) 321-9221

The Chicago Coalition for School Choice
P.O. Box 46122
Chicago, IL 60646
(312) 763-9292

COMMIT
P.O. Box 80252
Indianapolis, IN 46280-0252
(317) 580-8160

Hope for Ohio's Children
807 Society Building
159 S. Main Street
Akron, OH 44308
(800) 827-HOPE

Education Reform Groups

Indiana Policy Review Foundation
320 North Meridian
Suite 615
Indianapolis, IN 46204-1725
(317) 236-7360

The Mackinac Center
P.O. Box 568
119 Ashman Street
Midland, MI 48640
(517) 631-0900

Metanoia
554 Little Canada Road
St. Paul, MN 55117
(612) 484-1854

**National Association of Charter
Schools, Inc.**
The Charter School Chronicle
2722 E. Michigan, Suite 201
Lansing, MI 48912
(517) 772-9115

Resource Institute of Oklahoma
5101 North Classen Boulevard
Suite 307
Oklahoma City, OK 73118-4422
(405) 840-3005

**TEACH Michigan and
The Michigan Center for Charter Schools**
913 W. Holmes Street
Suite 265
Lansing, MI 48910
(517) 394-4870

Wisconsin Policy Research Institute
3107 North Shepard Avenue
Milwaukee, WI 53211-3135
(414) 963-0600

SOUTHWEST

Arizona Association of Charter Schools
2421 East Isabella
Mesa, AZ 85204
(602) 497-5337

**Arizona Institute for Public Policy
Research**
7000 North 16th Street
#120-420
Phoenix, AZ 85020
(602) 277-8682

Barry Goldwater Institute
Bank One Center—Concourse
201 North Central Avenue
Phoenix, AZ 85004
(602) 256-7018

**Texas Coalition for Parental
Choice in Education**
7707 Fannin
Suite 153
Houston, TX 77054
(713) 797-1776

Texas Justice Foundation
8122 Datapoint Drive
Suite 906
San Antonio, TX 78229
(210) 614-7157

Texas Public Policy Foundation
8122 Datapoint Drive
Suite 910
San Antonio, TX 78229
(210) 614-0080

PACIFIC AND THE NORTHWEST

Cascade Institute
813 SW Alder
Suite 707
Portland, OR 97205
(503) 242-0900

Center for Educational Change
3957 E. Burnside
Portland, OR 97214-0201
(503) 234-4600

The Claremont Institute
250 West First Street
Suite 330
Claremont, CA 91711
(909) 621-6825

Colorado Children's Campaign
1600 Sherman B-300
Denver, CO 80203
(303) 839-1580

Colorado League of Charter Schools
7700 W. Woodard Dr.
Lakewood, CO 80227
(303) 939-5356

Independence Institute
14142 Denver West Parkway
185
Golden, CO 80401
(303) 279-6536

Nevada Policy Research Institute
PO Box 20312
Reno, NV 89515-0312
(702) 786-9600

Pacific Research Institute
755 Sansome Street
Suite 450
San Francisco, CA 94111
(415) 989-0833

Reason Foundation
2125 Oak Grove Road
Suite 120
Walnut Creek, CA 94598
(510) 930-6027

School Futures Research
7730 Hershel Ave.
Suite F
Lajolla, CA 92037
(619) 459-2177

Washington Institute for Policy Studies
999 Third Avenue
#1060
Seattle, WA 98104
(206) 467-9561

Service Organizations*

Big Brothers/Big Sisters of America
230 North 13th Street
Philadelphia, PA 19107
(215) 567-7000

B'nai B'rith International
1640 Rhode Island Ave., NW
Washington, DC 20036
(202) 857-6600

Boys and Girls Clubs of America
1230 West Peachtree Street, NW
Atlanta, GA 30309
(404) 815-5757

Boy Scouts of America
345 Hudson
New Yory, NY 10014
(212) 242-1100

Camp Fire Girls and Boys
4601 Madison Avenue
Kansas City, MO 64112
(816) 756-0258

Center for Workforce Preparation
U.S. Chamber of Commerce
1615 H Street, NW
Washington, DC 20062
(202) 463-5525

Girl Scouts of the U.S.A
420 Fifth Avenue
New York, NY 10018-2702
(212) 852-8000

Girls Incorporated
3 East 33rd Street
New York, NY 10018-2702
(212) 683-1253

Kiwanis International National Headquarters
3636 Woodview Drive
Indianapolis, IN 46268-1168
(317) 875-8755

Knights of Columbus
1 Columbus Plaza
New Haven, CT 06507
(203) 772-2130

Lions Clubs International
300 22nd St.
Oak Brook, IL 60521
(708) 571-5466

National Urban League
1111 14th Street,NW
Suite 600
Washington, DC 20005
(202) 898-1604

Optimists International
4494 Lindell Boulevard
St. Louis, MO 63108-2498
(314) 371-6000

Rotary National Headquarters
1560 Sherman Avenue
Evanston, IL 60201
(708) 866-3000

U.S. Jaycess
P.O.Box 7
4W. 21st St.
Tulsa, OK 74102-0007
(918) 584-2481

YMCA of the USA
726 Broadway
New York, NY 10003
(212) 614-2700

*Many states and communities have their own unique service and fraternal organizations. Consult local directories.

Accountability: Responsibility for results, including the negative consequences of poor results.

Achievement Test: Test given to measure how much and how well a student has learned, either in a specific subject or skill, or overall, as pegged to an established scale of proficiency.

Assessment: The measurement of one's mastery over a subject or range of subjects; testing.

At-Risk: Students in danger of dropping out of school due to poor academic performance, truancy, behavioral problems or other conditions which may adversely affect their commitment to learning, such as chemical dependency or pregnancy.

Authentic Assessment: Test that measures a student's ability to apply learning in "real world" situations. This is a relatively new concept in practice, and is not widely accepted.

Basic Skills Test or Minimum Competency Test: Test given to measure a student's mastery of fundamental skills, in reading, writing and mathematics, appropriate for a certain grade level or for high school graduation.

Benchmark, or Benchmark Performance: A level of performance set as the standard against which a student's performance is measured and reported. Specific benchmarks are set from the lowest to highest levels of performance.

Bilingual Education: Schooling in which students who don't speak English are taught in both English and their native language. Such programs are designed to help students maintain their grade level in subjects as they learn English, but some believe that this delays their mastery of English and actually inhibits their mastery of other subjects as well.

Board of Education: At the state level, a body of officials responsible for determining various aspects of education policy for the state, such as curriculum and textbook selection. Depending on the state, they are either elected or appointed by the governor or legislature. They work with the governor, the legislature, the state's education department and superintendent. The school board is a similar body organized at the local, or district, level. (For more information see Chapter 6.)

Bond Referendum: Question put to a district's voters on whether the school district can issue bonds to fund the school; the bonds are repaid automatically through the district's tax levy.

Central Office: Administrative offices of the school district, superintendent and the school board.

Chapter One or Title One: Federal funds allocated to programs and districts that serve large concentrations of children from low-income, disadvantaged families.

Charter School: An independent public school that is freed from many local and state regulations and is instead held accountable for reaching and maintaining the student achievement goals approved in its charter. (For more information see Chapter 2.)

Chief State School Officer: The chief administrator of public education at the state level, generally going under the title of Superintendent or Commissioner. Depending on the state, the superintendent is either elected or is appointed by the governor or Board of Education. The superintendent heads the state department of education. (For more information see Chapter 7.)

Choice, or School Choice: A program in which parents are entitled to use the education tax-dollars allocated for their child to choose the best school for their child, regardless of whether the school is operated by a school district or independently. (For more information see Chapters 2 and 3.)

Consolidation: The practice of joining two or more school districts into one regional district, or several schools into one larger school, to create a single administrative or operational unit, presumably to benefit from economies of scale.

Cooperative or Collaborative Learning: Teaching method in which children work in groups to master a task, and the teacher takes on a moderating, rather than instructional role. Students are judged by how well they work in a group and the group's mastery of the task, rather than on their individual learning.

Desegregation: The process of determining school enrollments so that all racial groups are proportionately represented in each school. Many cities' schools are operating under court-ordered desegregation, in which a judge has ruled that the city must desegregate its schools, often through forced busing and magnet schools.

Dropout Rate: The number of students who leave high school without graduating and without enrolling in an alternative school.

Full Choice: School choice that includes traditional and non-traditional public schools and private and parochial schools.

Goals 2000: A federally funded program that establishes eight national education goals designed to raise student standards and achievement, and ties states' access to those funds to compliance with various federal guidelines.

Head Start: Federally funded program for preschool children from low-income families, intended to better prepare them for entry into kindergarten and elementary school.

Inclusion or Mainstreaming: The practice of placing children with physical, mental or emotional handicaps in regular classrooms, rather than in special education classes.

Inter-district Choice: Public school choice limited to selected school districts.

Intra-district Choice or Transfers: Public school choice limited to the schools within a district.

Magnet School: A school offering special vocational or academic programs designed to attract students from outside the school's traditional enrollment area. Most magnets are created to satisfy court-ordered desegregation orders; others are created to offer students specialized programs or alternative educational opportunities. (For more information see Chapter 2.)

Merit or Performance-Based Pay: Teacher compensation or bonuses based on a teacher's competency and achievement in the classroom, rather than on tenure, seniority or level of education.

Minimum Competency Test: See BASIC SKILLS TEST.

National Assessment of Educational Progress (NAEP): A standardized test designed and used by the National Assessment Governing Board to measure student achievement in various subjects in grades three, seven and eleven, for evaluation and comparison on a state and national level.

National Assessment Governing Board (NAGB): An independent bipartisan board, composed of state and local officials, educators and the public, that sets policy for NAEP.

Normed or Norm-referenced Assessment: Student achievement test that is scored against the performance of a particular sub-group of peers, rather than against a general standard. Tests can be normed by race, family income level, place of residence or other social factors that are often used to explain poor performance.

Open Enrollment or Public School Choice: State law or policy that allows parents to send their child to any public school in the state, or within certain defined parameters.

Open Meetings Act (Sunshine Law): Law requiring official public bodies such as school boards and boards of education to publicize their meetings and hold them open to the public, and provide public access to certain records.

Outcome Based Education (OBE): A controversial curriculum program that focuses on students mastering and exhibiting particular behaviors (outcomes) rather than subject content. Often includes collaborative learning, in which each child in a group must work on the task until all have mastered it; children are retested until they achieve a certain level of mastery. OBE is said to foster cooperation, rather than competitiveness, but often leads to a slowing and watering down of the curriculum.

Parental Choice Grant or Voucher: A monetary grant which is given to qualifying parents from the district or state to pay for their child's school costs at a public or private school. The amount of the grant is based in whole or part on local public school costs. The grant is given directly to the parents and they redeem it at the school of their choice. (For more information see Chapters 2 and 3.)

Portfolio Assessment: A more subjective measurement of a child's academic achievement based on work assignments and teacher observation rather than solely on periodic achievement tests.

Performance-Based Pay: See MERIT PAY.

Post-Secondary Enrollment Option: A school choice program in which high school students may opt to attend college classes, rather than high school classes, to earn credits and grades simultaneously toward high school graduation and college.

Private Contracting: The hiring by a school district of a private company to operate some or all of the schools in the district, to provide specific academic programs, such as remedial, at-risk, or special education, or to teach certain parts of a curriculum, such as foreign language, science, or math. Districts also contract out for support services including transportation, food services, maintenance and administration. (For more information see Chapter 2.)

Private Scholarship Programs: School choice programs set up by private corporations or foundations to provide low-income parents with tuition assistance to send their children to the public, private or parochial school of their choice. (For more information see Chapter 2.)

Public Hearing: A meeting on school policy or other taxpayer issues to which the public is invited to attend for information and to voice their views.

Public School Choice: See OPEN ENROLLMENT.

Regional District: A district formed by two or more neighboring school districts in order to consolidate the delivery of particular programs. For example, a regional district high school might serve students from a number of elementary school districts.

Remediation or Remedial Education: Additional instruction given outside the regular school curriculum to help students who have fallen behind in or lack specific skills needed for their grade-level course work.

Scholastic Assessment Test (SAT): Widely used and recognized standardized test used to measure a student's mastery of verbal and mathematics skills considered appropriate for high school students (formerly the Scholastic Aptitude Test). Many colleges use SAT scores as

one indication of a student's readiness for college-level work. Colleges in some states, particularly those in the west, may instead use a similar test called American College Testing, or ACT.

School Board: At the district level, citizens elected to set and administer the school budget and education policy for the district (in three percent of districts the board is appointed). They generally hire, and work with, the district superintendent in the central office. (For more information see Chapter 6.)

School Choice: See CHOICE.

School District: A geographically determined governmental unit established to oversee the provision of education to the area's residence. A district may operate schools itself or contract out for such services.

Site-Based or School-Based Management (SBM): Management of certain aspects of a school's operation by a school site council made up teachers, parents, administrators and community members. Such councils rarely have sufficient authority to significantly change the way a district school operates.

Social Promotion: The practice of passing a student on to the next grade level based on age rather than achievement.

Special Education: Programs designed to serve the educational needs of mentally, physically or emotionally handicapped students.

Standard: The level of learning appropriate for a student as determined by a school, district or other entity.

Standardized Test: Test that is administered and scored in exactly the same way for all students, with levels of achievement set against the results of previous test-takers. Standardized tests like the SAT and NAEP are used to provided information on the general level of United States student achievement in individual states and overall.

Student (or Pupil) / Staff Ratio: For a school, district or state, the average number of students per each professional employee, including teachers, counselors, librarians and administrators.

Student (or Pupil) / Teacher Ratio: For a school, district or state, the average number of students in a classroom per each teacher.

Superintendent: Chief administrative officer of a school district, usually appointed by the district school board. The term also applies to the chief state school officer. (For more information see Chapter 6.)

Tax Levy Referendum: A question put before a district's voters on whether to make changes to the tax levies currently funding the district's schools.

Teachers Union: A labor organization to which teachers pay dues in return for the union's negotiation of labor contracts with the school district. Teachers unions' activities can extend beyond collective bargaining to the influence of other school policies and often to the exercise of political lobbying activities. (For more information see Chapter 5.)

Tenure: The practice of guaranteeing a teacher's employment after a certain number of years (generally about three) working in a pub-

lic school or district. It is very difficult for a district to fire a tenured teacher.

Tuition Tax Credit: A method by which parents can deduct a certain amount of their child's school tuition directly from the amount of taxes they owe.

Tuition Tax Deduction: A deduction parents can take, based on their child's school tuition, to reduce the amount of income on which they must pay taxes.

Voucher: See PARENTAL CHOICE GRANT.

APPENDIX IV: SUGGESTED READING AND RESOURCE LIST

Allen, Jeanne. *School Reform in the United States: State by State Summary,* Washington, D.C.: The Center for Education Reform, updated periodically.

Bennett, William J. *Our Children & Our Country,* New York, New York: Simon & Schuster, 1988.

Bigler, Philip and Lockard, Karen. *Failing Grades: A Teacher's Report Card on Education in America,* Arlington, Virginia: Vandamere Press, 1992.

Charter School Resource Center. *The Massachusetts Charter School Handbook,* Boston, Massachusetts: Pioneer Institute for Public Policy Research, 1994.

Chubb, John E. and Moe, Terry M. *Politics, Markets & America's Schools,* Washington, DC: The Brookings Institution, 1990.

Doyle, Denis P. and Hartle, Terry W. *Excellence in Education: The States Take Charge,* Washington, D.C.: American Enterprise Institute for Public Policy Research, 1985.

Finn, Chester E. *We Must Take Charge,* New York, New York: The Free Press, 1991.

Fliegel, Sy. *Miracle in East Harlem: The Fight for Choice in Public Schools,* New York, New York: Times Books, 1993.

Halpern, Keith A. and Culbertson, Eliza R. *Blueprint for Change: Charter Schools, A Handbook for Action,* Washington, DC: Democratic Leadership Council, 1994.

Hansen, Barbara J. and Mackey, Philip E. *Your Public Schools: What You Can Do to Help Them,* North Haven, Connecticut: Catbird Press, 1993.

Hanushek, Eric A. *Making Schools Work,* Washington, DC: The Brookings Institution, 1994.

Hill, Paul T., Foster, Gail E., and Gendler, Tamar. *High Schools With Character,* Santa Monica, California: The RAND Corporation.

Hirsch, E.D. *Cultural Literacy,* New York, New York: Random House, 1988.

Kearns, David and Doyle, Denis. *Winning the Brain Race,* San Francisco, California: Institute for Contemporary Studies Press, 1988.

Kilpatrick, William. *Why Johnny Can't Tell Right From Wrong,* New York, New York: Simon & Schuster, 1992.

Kramer, Rita. *Ed School Follies: The Miseducation of America's Teachers*, New York, New York: The Free Press, 1991.

Lieberman, Myron. *Public Education: An Autopsy*, London, England: Harvard University Press, 1993.

Nathan, Joe. *Free to Teach*, Cleveland, Ohio: Pilgrim Press.

National Center for Education Statistics. *The Condition of Education*, Washington, D.C.: U.S. Department of Education, published annually.

Ravitch, Diane and Finn, Chester E. *What Do Our 17-Year-Olds Know?* New York, New York: Harper & Row, 1987.

Sizer, Theodore R. *Horace's Compromise: The Dilemma of the American High School*, Boston, Massachusetts: Houghton Mifflin Company, 1984.

Sowell, Thomas. *Inside American Education: the Decline, the Deception, the Dogmas*, New York, New York: Free Press/Macmillan Script, 1992.

Toch, Thomas. *In the Name of Excellence: The Struggle to Reform the Nation's Schools, Why It's Failing and What Should Be Done*, New York, New York: Oxford University Press, 1991.

Introduction

[1]National Center for Education Statistics, *Public High School Graduates, 1990-1, Compared With Ninth Grade Enrollment in Fall 1987,* (Washington, D.C.: U.S. Department of Education, December 13, 1993).

[2]*Goals 2000* Educate America Act, p.115.

[3]Kirsch, Irwin S.; Jungeblut, Ann; and Kolstad, Andrew. *Adult Literacy in America: A First Look at the Results of the National Adult Literacy Survey,* (Washington, D.C.: Educational Testing Service, September 1993).

[4]National Center for Education Statistics, *Public High School Graduates, 1990-1, Compared With Ninth Grade Enrollment in Fall 1987,* (Washington, D.C.: U.S. Department of Education, December 13, 1993).

[5]Elam, Stanley M., Rose, Lowell C., and Gallup, Alec M. *The 26th Annual Phi Delta Kappa Gallup Poll of the Public's Attitudes Toward the Public Schools,* (Bloomington, IN: Phi Delta Kappa, September 1994).

Section I

Chapter 1

[1]National Commission on Excellence in Education, *A Nation at Risk: The Imperative for Educational Reform,* (Washington, D.C.: U.S. Government Printing Office, 1983), p. 5.

[2]See Appendix IV: Suggested Reading and Resource List.

[3]Fliegel, Sy. *Miracle in East Harlem: The Fight for Choice in Public Schools,* (New York, NY: Times Books, 1993).

[4]Allen, Jeanne. *School Reform in the United States: State by State Summary,* (Washington, D.C.: The Center for Education Reform, Summer 1994), pp. 7-8.

[5]Institute for Justice, "Puerto Rico School Choice Program," September 20,1994.

[6]States with charter school laws granting more freedom from regulations: Arizona, Massachusetts, Michigan, Minnesota, California, and Colorado. States with laws granting less freedom: Hawaii, Georgia, Kansas, New Mexico, and Wisconsin.

[7]Bowman, Craig. "There Are No Shortcuts in Education," *The Denver Post,* November 3, 1994.

[8]National Center for Education Statistics. *Public High School Graduates, 1990-91, Compared with ninth Grade Enrollment in Fall 1987,* (Washington, D.C.: U.S. Department of Education, December 13, 1993).

[9]Goals 2000 Educate America Act, p. 115.

[10]National Center for Education Statistics. *The Condition of Education 1993,* (Washington, D.C.: U.S. Department of Education, 1993), p. 58.

[11]National Center for Education Statistics. *The Condition of Education 1994*, (Washington, D.C.: U.S. Department of Education, 1994), p. 34.

[12]National Center for Education Statistics. *Youth Indicators 1993: Trends in the Well Being of American Youth*, (Washington, D.C.: U.S. Department of Education, 1993).

[13]National Center for Education Statistics. *The Condition of Education 1993*, (Washington, D.C.: U.S. Department of Education, 1993), p. 58.

[14]National Education Commission on Time and Learning. *Prisoners of Time*, (Washington, D.C.: U.S. Government Printing Office, April 1994), p. 7.

[15]National Education Commission on Time and Learning. *Prisoners of Time*, (Washington, D.C.: U.S. Government Printing Office, April 1994), pp. 24-5.

[16]ENational Center for Education Statistics. *The Condition of Education 1993*, (Washington, D.C.: U.S. Department of Education, 1993), p. 128.

[17]American Legislative Exchange Council. *Report Card on American Education 1994*, (Washington, D.C.: ALEC, September 1994), p. 6.

[18]"SAT Averages by State," *Education Daily*, August 28, 1994.

[19]National Center for Education Statistics. *The Condition of Education 1994*, (Washington, D.C.: U.S. Department of Education, 1994), p. 225.

[20]National Education Goals Panel. *The National Education Goals Report: Building a Nation of Learners 1994*, (Washington, D.C.: U.S. Government Printing Office, 1994), p. 35.

[21]Kirsch, Irwin S.; Jungeblut, Ann; Jenkins, Lynn; and Kolstad, Andrew. *Adult Literacy in America: A First Look at the Results of the National Adult Literacy Survey*, (Washington, D.C.: National Center for Education Statistics, 1993).

[22]U.S. Department of Education. *Executive Summary of the NAEP 1992, Mathematics Report Card for the Nation and the States*, (Washington, D.C.: U.S. Government Printing Office, April 1993), p. 2.

[23]U.S. Department of Education. *Executive Summary of the NAEP 1992, Mathematics Report Card for the Nation and the States*, (Washington, D.C.: U.S. Government Printing Office, April 1993), pp. 1-4.

[24]Finn, Chester and Ravitch, Diane. *What Do Our 17-Year-Olds Know?* (New York, NY: Harper & Row, 1987).

[25]The Center for Education Reform publishes materials tracking various education reforms around the nation, including: *School Reform in the United States: State by State Summary*.

Chapter 2

[1]*Arkansas Democrat Gazette*, October 24, 1994.

[2]Ibid.

[3]Ibid.

[4]Malone, Mike; Nathan, Joe; and Sedio, Darryl. *Facts, Figures and Faces: A Look at Minnesota's School Choice Programs*, (Minneapolis, MN: Center for School Change, November 1993).

[5]"On the Wild Side: New York City's Wildcat Academy," *New York Times*, July 11, 1994.

[6]"Prison or Phoenix Academy: The Choice is Theirs," *New York Times*, July 12, 1994.

[7]Association for Supervision and Curriculum Development. "School-Based Management: Pluses and Minuses," *UPDATE*, September 1994.

[8]Adapted from: Kolderie, Ted. *A Model Charter Schools Bill*, (Saint Paul, MN: Center for Policy Studies, 1994).

[9]Dale, Angela H. *Charter Schools: The New Neighborhood Schools*, (Washington, D.C.: The Center for Education Reform, March 1995).

[10]Wallis, Claudia. "A Class of Their Own," *Time Magazine*, October 31, 1994, p.54-55.

[11]Richardson, Joan. "MEA Seeks War Chest in Fighting School Plan," *Detroit Free Press*, November 5, 1993.

[12]Malone, Mike; Nathan, Joe; and Sedio, Darryl. *Facts, Figures and Faces: A Look at Minnesota's School Choice Programs*, (Minneapolis, MN: Center for School Change, November 1993).

[13]Beales, Janet and O'Leary, John. *Making Schools Work: Contracting Options for Better Management*, (San Francisco, CA: Reason Foundation, November 1993), p. 15.

[14]Cushman, Jennifer. "District School Board Gets Education on Privatization," *Chandler Independent*, February 5, 1992.

[15]"Contracting Out: Strategies for Fighting Back," *NEA Manual*, 1993.

[16]For more information call: Options for Youths, 2529 Foothill Boulevard, Suite 1, Lacrescenta, CA 91214, (818)542-3555.

[17]"Ombudsman Bid in Texas," *Ombudsman Educational Services Outlook*, Fall 1994.

[18]"Raise Your Hand: Test Your Ombudsman I.Q.," *Ombudsman Educational Services Outlook*, Fall 1994.

[19]Education Alternatives, Inc., *Schools That Work*, (Minneapolis, MN: EAI, 1994).

[20]McGroarty, Daniel. "School Choice Slandered," *The Public Interest*, Number 117, Fall 1994.

[21]Allen, Jeanne. "Making Educational Reform a Reality," *Alternatives in Philanthropy*, (Washington, D.C.: Capital Research Center, October 1994).

[22]Parental testimony was obtained from: Austin CEO Foundation, "Has the Scholarship You Received Last Year From the CEO Made a Difference for Your Child?" *Press Release*, 1994.

[23]Blasor, Lorraine. "300 Families Await Ruling on Vouchers," *San Juan Star*, August 9, 1994.

[23]Institute for Justice, "Puerto Rico School Choice Program," September 20, 1994.

Chapter 3

[1]Topolnicki, Denise M. "Why Private Schools Are Rarely Worth the Money," *Money Magazine*, October 1994.

[2]Editorial. "Put Schools Before Rules," *Boston Globe*, June 22, 1994.

[3]Bannockburn Civic Association. "New Math? Robot Replaces Human Teacher at Whitman," *Bannockburn Newsletter*, November 1994.

[4]Asimov, Nanette. "Lessons for California; How Vouchers Work in Milwaukee," *San Francisco Chronicle*, September 27, 1993.

[5]Beales, Janet. "Offering Parents a Real School Choice," *The Washington Times*, May 22, 1994.

[6]Mathews, Jay. "Upgrading a Big School By Breaking It Down," *The Washington Post*, August 26,1994.

[7]Brown, DeNeen L. "Parents Lash Out During Hearing on D.C. Schools," *Washington Post*, September 25, 1994.

[8]Feldman, Carol. "Civil Rights Leaders Wear Scars of Controversy," *Washington Times*, May 17, 1994.

[9]Shogren, Elizabeth. "A Chance to See Choice at Work; Milwaukee is the Only City That Uses Public Vouchers for Private Schools," *Los Angeles Times*, October 22, 1993.

[10]Schuster, Beth and Chavez, Stephanie. "Law Starts School Shopping Frenzy, Education Open Enrollment Prompts Families to Pore Over Options. Some Take Another Look at Public Schools," *Los Angeles Times*, March 26,1994.

[11]Institute for Justice. "Puerto Rico School Choice Program," September 20,1994.

[12]Billingsley, K. L., ed. *Voices on Choice: The Education Reform Debate*, (San Francisco, CA: Pacific Research Institute for Public Policy, 1994), pp. 1-10.

Section II

Chapter 4

[1]Wallis, Claudia. "A Class of Their Own," *Time*, October 31, 1994, p. 54.

[2]Letter, *Valley Views Newspaper*, (Danville, California).

Chapter 5

[1]For a comprehensive look at the structure, budget and political activity of the NEA and the AFT, see Haar, Charlene; Lieberman, Myron; and Troy, Leo. *The NEA and the AFT: Teacher Unions in Power and Politics*, (London, England: Harvard University Press, 1994).

[2]Dillion, Sam. "Teachers and Tenure: Rights Versus Discipline," *New York Times*, June 28,1994.

[3]National Education Association, "The 1994 Election Results: Challenges for NEA," NEA Literature.

[4]Lambro, Donald, "Despite Loss at Polls in California, School Choice Movement is Not Dead," *The Atlanta Journal and Constitution*, November 17, 1993.

[5]Richardson, Joan, "MEA Seeks War Chest in Fighting School Plan," *Detroit Free Press*, November 5, 1993.

[6]Palutis, Annette and Matino, Carmen J. "Alert to Mobilize for Public Education," *PSEA Internal Memo*, January 14, 1994.

● ●

Chapter 6

[1]"Political Skills Can Help You Avoid 'Board Burnout'," *School Board News/Conference Edition*, April 10, 1994.
"Avoid Personal Liability," *School Board News/Conference Edition*, April 10, 1994.
"TV News Must Do a Better Job, Gumbel Urges," *School Board News/Conference Edition*, April 11, 1994.
"Education Essential For Free Trade," *School Board News/Conference Edition*, April 12, 1994.

[2]*National School Boards Association Conference*, 1994.

[3]"How Teachers Erase Boards," *Wall Street Journal*, April 18, 1994.

[4]Haar, Charlene; Lieberman, Myron; and Troy, Leo. *The NEA and the AFT: Teacher Unions in Power and Politics*, (London, England: Harvard University Press, 1994), p. 13.

[5]Bainbridge, William L. "Revisiting the 'Folly'," *SCHOOL and COLLEGE*, February 1994.

[6]Lindsay, Drew. "Educators Buck Giving the Public Its Say on Taxes," *Education Week*, November 2, 1994.

[7]Schmidt, Peter. "Illinois State Board Moves to Take Over Troubled East St. Louis Schools," *Education Week*, October 26,1994.

[8]Editorial. *Boston Globe*, June 22, 1994.

[9]Watson, Jacqueline. "Good Teachers, Bad Teachers Put the Sacred Cow of Tenure Out to Pasture," *San Diego Union-Tribune*, March 2,1994.

Chapter 7

[1]U.S. Department of Education, "Connecting Families and Schools: Building Partnerships That Work," *Satellite Town Meeting*, November 1994.

[2]Feldman, Carol. "Civil Rights Leaders Wear Scars of Controversy," *Washington Times*, May 17,1994.

Chapter 9

[1]National Education Association, "Getting Ready for the Right," *Advocacy Action*.

[2]*NEA Today*, April 1994.

[3]National Education Association, "Getting Ready for the Right," *Advocacy Action*.

Section III

Chapter 10

[1]Finn, Chester. *Public Perspective* Interview, Winter 1993.

[2]Finn, Chester. *We Must Take Charge: Our Schools and Our Future*, (New York, NY: The Free Press, 1991), p. 263.

[3]Sack, Kevin. "Curbs Approved For Custodians in Public Schools," *New York Times*, November 17, 1993.

● ●

⁴Hansen, Barbara J. and Mackey, Philip E. *Your Public Schools: What You Can Do to Help Them*, (North Haven, CT: Catbird Press, 1993).

⁵See Appendix II resources for address and telephone number.

⁶See Appendix II for listing.

⁷Texas Education Agency, *Texas Public School Statistics*, (TX: TEA, 1994).

Chapter 11

¹Weil, Nancy. "Parent Starting Group to Monitor Schools," *St. Petersburg Times*, May 3,1994.

²Hansen, Barbara J. and Mackey, Philip E. *Your Public Schools: What You Can Do to Help Them*, (North Haven, CT: Catbird Press, 1993).

Chapter 14

¹Portions of "Communicating with your State Representative" were adapted from: Smith, Daniel C. Attorney at Law, *Guidelines for Getting Involved in Legislative Decisions*.

Index

is a publication of *The Center for Education Reform,*
a non-profit, national clearinghouse that is

"... making schools work better for all children."

If you are interested in additional copies or further information about Center activities,
publications or resources, write or call:

1001 Connecticut Ave., NW
Suite #920
Washington, DC 20036
(202) 822-9000

or dial our **Helpline** at **(800) 521-2118**
Be sure to ask about group rates